COMBAT LEADER TO CORPORATE LEADER

COMBAT LEADER TO CORPORATE LEADER

20 Lessons to Advance Your Civilian Career

Chad Storlie

 PRAEGER

AN IMPRINT OF ABC-CLIO, LLC
Santa Barbara, California • Denver, Colorado • Oxford, England

Library of Congress Cataloging-in-Publication Data

Storlie, Chad.
   Combat leader to corporate leader : 20 lessons to advance your civilian career / Chad Storlie.
      p. cm.
   Includes bibliographical references and index.
      ISBN 978-0-313-38332-8 (alk. paper) — ISBN 978-0-313-38333-5 (e-book)
   1. Veterans—Employment—United States. 2. Veterans—Vocational guidance—United States. 3. Job hunting—United States. 4. Career changes—United States. I. Title.
      UB357.S83 2010
      658.4'09—dc22   2010006679

ISBN: 978-0-313-38332-8
EISBN: 978-0-313-38333-5

14 13 12 11 10   1 2 3 4 5

This book is also available on the World Wide Web as an eBook.
Visit www.abc-clio.com for details.

Praeger
An Imprint of ABC-CLIO, LLC

ABC-CLIO, LLC
130 Cremona Drive, P.O. Box 1911
Santa Barbara, California 93116-1911

This book is printed on acid-free paper ∞
Manufactured in the United States of America

There are three groups of people who made this book possible.

The first is my wife, Deborah, who supported me when everything was an idea and then made everything possible.

The second are my two sons, Aaron and Connor. They bring the greatest joy with the smallest actions.

The third are the soldiers who made me into the officer that I am today. Everyone in the military owes a debt to those who made him or her into a great soldier, and I am no exception. This book is a partial repayment to those who took the time to make me a good officer. May each of them have a great second career.

CONTENTS

Preface: The Military Veteran and Re-Entering the Civilian World[1]

This is a book about how to apply the best aspects of military service and leverage those military skills to succeed in a civilian career. The path from a successful military career to a successful civilian career is a sometimes complex and occasionally disappointing route. Above all, the transition from the military into the civilian world is not one that should be taken lightly. On top of the change in military culture and traditions to the varied employment culture of civilian employment, there is the difficulty of the transition from combat to peace. However, in spite of all the challenges, veterans every day are able to bring the full value of their military experiences back to the civilian world.

The transition from combat to a peacetime environment is complex, long, and usually frustrating to one degree or another. The combat veteran will be undergoing two large transitions at the same time: (1) the transition from combat to peace, and (2) the transition from the military employment culture to the civilian employment culture. Undertaking these two transitions simultaneously is quite challenging and calls for a great deal of structure, understanding, and confidence to do it correctly. Before jumping into the workforce, the world of education, or another pursuit, the military veteran should pause to consider some options. Below is a list of topics designed to provide structure and guidance to help military veterans succeed in their next chosen path.

What Are Your Plan and Goals?

The military provides a great deal of daily social and work-life structure. The fact that military life is so structured—PT, breakfast, training, work details, etc.—actually helps reduce a great deal of post-deployment stress because, even after the return from combat, there is a daily structure to life to help guide you. Even for the most senior military veterans, there is a whirlwind of change and a complete lack of structure once they are released from active duty and return to the civilian world. Freedom is a great thing, but too much unstructured time can be a downfall that leads to too much TV, video games, overeating, alone time, alcohol, or other types of risky behavior. As a military veteran, you'll need to make a plan to create structure and discipline in daily life so you do not lose focus on your goals. Create a list of what you want to do: exercise, see friends, sit in on classes at a college, take a part-time job, start a small business, or engage in a constructive hobby such as photography or walking a section of the Appalachian Trail. Having a daily structure built around goals, things that you enjoy, and people that support you makes the combat-to-civilian transition immensely easier. Finally, take a pause every few weeks to assess how your return is progressing and whether anything needs to change.

What Is Your Story to the World?

Military veterans of the past 20 years make up about 1.5% of the U.S. population. A recent military veteran, especially a combat veteran, will be a rarity in U.S. society and will inevitably run into questions like "Did you have to kill anyone? What were the people of Afghanistan like? Was the local food any good? Where in the world is Iraq? Are we still in Iraq and Afghanistan?" (That's my personal favorite.) It is best to have a set of practiced responses to these seemingly disrespectful and uninformed questions. A practiced response will help you navigate these perhaps-innocent questions instead of becoming angry or despondent over what may appear to be people's lack of concern. The vast majority of civilians are exceptionally proud of the military and the performance of the military in combat in Iraq and Afghanistan. A prepared story that is simple and well described, and that contains some humorous anecdotes, will greatly help you explain your time in combat and make you more comfortable explaining your experiences in the military. This will not close the experience gap, but it will make the recent military veteran more at ease explaining his or her time serving the country to an audience that knows very little about the military. This ability to bridge experience gaps is essential for anyone involved in business, education, or other professions.

Take Some Time to Explore All Your Options

The literal and immediate descent from combat to the civilian world is very disorienting. You need to structure your daily time to retain vital military discipline, but you also need to "loosen up" and take some time to explore the world that you have been away from. Travel, programs such as Outward Bound, starting a small business with minimal to no capital investment, or taking a few college classes prior to full-time enrollment are excellent ways to try things out, explore, and make sure that your next path in life is one that you want. Immediately going from combat to the civilian world, to a job or the college classroom, can at times be too much. Take three to six months to get comfortable and explore your options before jumping into a new career or educational path, to make your combat-to-civilian transition a success.

Understand the Daily Risks to a Recently Returned Military Veteran

From your first step off the plane, you know that in the newfound freedom of the civilian world, there are plenty of things that can derail your plans for the future. Alcohol, drug use, fast cars and motorcycles, men and women more interested in your bank account than you, and personal financial mismanagement are just a few of the dangers to which recent military combat veterans have succumbed. Recent veterans must accept that the transition from combat to the civilian world will be difficult, and that there will be residual effects from combat exposure such as combat stress, the potential for PTSD, the inability to easily relax, a distance from "normal" people that will eventually dissipate, and that "funny" feeling when you are out and about without a weapon or in a large crowd. The use of counseling programs, veteran-to-veteran conversation, exercise, a good diet, yoga, and programs that teach stress-mitigation techniques all help reduce risky behavior and make for a much more successful transition. For me, exercise, no alcohol, breathing exercises, and visualization exercises were key in making the combat-to-civilian transition easier—and successful.

Don't Be Afraid to Ask for Help and to Help Others

You will be amazed at the literally hundreds of resources for military veterans undergoing the readjustment from combat. There are programs and people to help process VA claims, treat PTSD, provide assistance with employment, and aid veterans in the transition from combat to the classroom. Your military experience has made you a fantastic leader, so there is space to help with civilian volunteer organizations such as Habitat for Humanity, shelters for homeless veterans, and existing veteran service organizations. The ability to accept help and offer help to others is a skill that I have been amazed at in recent combat veterans. The key to both receiving and offering help is that the military veteran has to be willing to get involved. Getting involved in civilian society is vitally important to a successful transition.

A Successful Transition from Combat to the Future

You will build your own path from combat to peace. My steps and those of other recent combat veterans outline the procedures and advice that we used or wished we had known when we came back from combat. Combat veterans understand that combat has changed us, but all veterans seek to use the experience of combat, and what it taught us, to improve our daily lives and the lives of others. You have had different experiences than I have, or than the Marine next to me has had, but we can all leverage that experience to become better people and to ensure we have a fulfilling, successful career as well as a fulfilling, happy, and satisfying life.

Note

1. This preface is based on my letter to the editor that appeared in the August 2009 issue of *Army* magazine. Sections reprinted with permission.

ACKNOWLEDGMENTS

A book may be authored by one person, but it reflects the input, dedication, hard work, and support of many people. The first person I'd like to thank is my wife, Deborah, who embraced the idea of creating a framework to help military veterans transition to a more productive, higher-valued, and more fulfilling civilian career. Jeff Olson and all the staff at Praeger Publishers took a chance on a new idea to help veterans succeed, and listened to the ideas of an unknown author.

I have also had the benefit of a great many friends who read chapters of my book and offered feedback. This has made the book a better, more valuable guide to effective leadership for veterans. I would like to thank John Ruehlin, Michael Cygan, Kyle Privette, Brian Bartlett, Andrew Kletzing, Christina Hruska, Wesley Gray, Zachary Mundell, Brendan Kelley, William Boucek, Ryan Marsh, and Craig Monaghan for their direct feedback and valuable perspectives on draft chapters. A special thank-you to Robert Gonzales, a Marine Corps veteran, for his great graphic design work and suggestions.

In the Army, I prepared soldiers for battle. This book will help prepare all military veterans to be better and more valued in their civilian careers.

INTRODUCTION

As a military veteran on today's battlefield, you have been exposed to the highest levels of sustained combat since the Vietnam War. You may have been deployed to Iraq, Afghanistan, or both, and served two, three, or four combat zone tours. The war in Afghanistan, in its eighth year, and the war in Iraq, in its sixth year, have tested the endurance of the U.S. military and created a generation of Americans with unparalleled excellence and experience that will be used to build the value of American society.

As a veteran, you have battlefield experience, military training, personal passion, the inherent understanding of using intelligence to drive operational excellence, dedication to country and peers, and the ability to do and achieve what others would consider impossible. Veterans before you have fulfilled their service obligations and returned to corporations, government, farms, nonprofit organizations, charities, small businesses, and universities, to continue their contributions to what made and continues to make America great. This book, combined with your passion and military professionalism will help make you an even greater contributor to the business world and society.

The Challenges of the Workforce Landscape for Military Veterans

As you transition from the military, you will face challenges from a variety of factors, primarily the change from combat to the normality of the non-combat world. You will be confronted by (1) the absence of danger and the challenge of adjusting your body and mind to an environment that is safe, (2) the need to reshape your personal, family, and career perspectives to this new environment in order to be successful and happy, (3) the question of how to apply your previous military experiences and training to advance your new careers, and (4) a U.S. and global economy that is only beginning to demonstrate the possibility of emerging from a prolonged recession. Any one of these four factors would be enough to challenge a career transition, but all four together create a seemingly impenetrable wall in the way of successful employment and a successful civilian career. The bottom line for you is that you desire to be as successful in your new civilian career as you were in the military. Your unique skills sets from military service and training will help make you and other veterans into the future leaders of business, government, community, and society.

Rising Veteran Unemployment Rates Point to Under-Utilization of Military Veteran Employees

The trend for veteran employment is disheartening. Military veterans have sacrificed *more*, but are increasingly being recognized with rewarding employment far *less*. From 1995 to 2003, an eight-year period spanning little military action and a recession, veterans aged 20 to 24 years had an unemployment rate that was, on average, about 1.35 percentage points higher than their non-veteran counterparts of comparable age and equivalent education (see Figure I.1). Simply stated, veterans were only very slightly worse off in their macro-level employment condition than their non-veteran counterparts up until 2003.[1] However, beginning in 2003, after the U.S. military had seen the initial stages of fighting in Iraq and two years of combat in Afghanistan, veteran unemployment rates began to drastically outpace those of their civilian counterparts.

The military veteran age brackets most affected by unemployment were the 20- to 24-year-olds and the 25- to 34-year-olds.[2] These two age brackets comprise, on average, 65% of the U.S. military discharges that have occurred since 2000. Operation Iraqi Freedom and Operation Enduring Freedom veteran unemployment rates for ages 18 to 24 and 25 to 34 is, on average, 50% to 100% higher than for non-veterans. The overall trend for veteran unemployment continues to be worse than for the overall civilian pool. In August 2009, civilian unemployment sat at 9.7%, versus 11.3% for all veterans—approximately 20% worse.

In order to be successful in your second career, you must be able to bring your military training and experience to your civilian employment, so you can make a bigger impact within the business organization and increase your value to the organization. In the business world, the bigger the splash you make, the greater your chances of promotion and additional opportunity. A keystone for your success in business is to fully leverage all of your military training and experience in the corporate business world to make a bigger difference. Once you demonstrate your skills fully, the hiring marketplace for your skills will improve both inside and outside your company, even in a down economy.

Combat Leader to Corporate Leader will transform your ability to contribute constructively to the success of any organization. The purpose of the book is to enable military veterans to deliver valuable skills to all businesses, no matter the size. *Combat Leader to Corporate Leader* will help you apply your skills to a wide range of businesses. Your military skill sets and experiences can help businesses of any size, from 1 employee to 500,000.

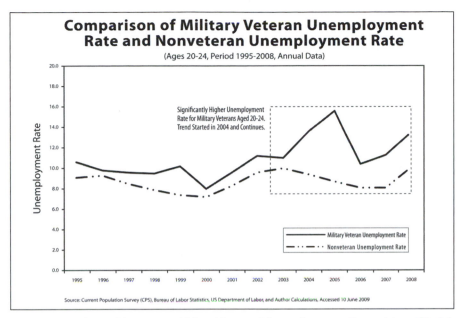

Figure I.1 Military Veteran and Non-Veteran Unemployment Rates (Ages 20–24, 1995–2008).

Realizing that Veteran Military Experience Can Play a Greater and More Productive Role in Business

My story as a military veteran returning from Iraq is nearly so "normal" that it does not bear distinction. In early 2004, after a year in Iraq as part of the initial ground invasion force, I struggled not only with how to transition from ground combat back to civilian society, but also how to apply my military skill sets to my new life as a commercial businessperson. The physical transition from combat to non-combat is ridiculously simple: In as little as six hours, you are back, sipping a German beer with the taste of sand still in your mouth and the dust of Baghdad still on your uniform. I remember drinking a beer in Rota, Spain, with six other bug-eyed, sleep-deprived, and shivering (the evening temperature was in the 70s, compared with the 90s we were used to) soldiers, all with our backs to the wall as we watched the sun come up over low hills while listening to the wail of Air Force transports arriving and departing. The seemingly near-instant physical transition from combat only makes the mental transition from combat harder for your mind.

What motivates and inspires me and other veterans is the promise of a new career, and opportunities to learn new things and to contribute again to the leadership and success of an organization. The drive to create, succeed, lead, and contribute is the central motivating force for veterans.

How You Can Make a Greater Difference to Your Organization

What steps can you take to maximize your experiences of combat and military training to establish, improve, and propel your continuing or new career after the military? Employers of veterans often look to them to solve big challenges and take on additional responsibilities, thanks to their "can-do" attitudes and performance-under-pressure skills. All veterans inherently recognize that the military-to-civilian transition is difficult, especially in the workplace. The key point of struggle is that recognizing the problem is not enough. Veterans need skills, tools, understandings, and approaches *today* to accelerate their careers and their employers' business results.

Combat Leader to Corporate Leader is not a book that directly compares combat to business. Combat is about killing the enemy, keeping your own forces alive with whatever effort necessary, minimizing destruction, imposing your will upon the enemy, and doing what it takes to win. On the opposite end of the spectrum, good business is the discovery, nurture, development, integration, and continuation of relationships that benefit both parties. *Combat Leader to Corporate Leader* is about using common military skill sets and planning principles in a way that will fully and quickly bring a commercial benefit to corporations and enable their employees to be better, more fulfilled, and more productive.

Organization of *Combat Leader to Corporate Leader*

Combat Leader to Corporate Leader is designed to be read either in a "choose your chapter" fashion or sequentially in its entirety. The goal of the book is to give veterans a set of tools and skill sets that will allow them to employ their military skills and experience to be able to overcome some of the most demanding business problems in the areas of leadership, competitive analysis, planning, employee development, risk management, safety, mentoring, avoiding workplace problems, and improving operations. *Combat Leader to Corporate Leader* was written for three primary audiences: (1) veterans, (2) the employers of veterans, and (3) non-veterans who wish to improve their business skill sets by adopting military skills that can be translated to business.

Combat Leader to Corporate Leader is divided into four sections that build upon the skill sets that every veteran has—regardless of your branch of service. The book follows the format of solving a problem following these four basic steps: (1) Understanding the business environment, (2) Planning an effective and achievable solution, (3) Executing the solution to meet the business objectives, and (4) Improving operations following execution, for more effective business operations. The understand-plan-execute-improve methodology is specifically designed to mirror the process U.S. military forces use to prepare for operations through the work of intelligence gathering (understand), mission planning (plan), conducting operations (execute), and performing post-operation assessments (improve).

The purpose of *Combat Leader to Corporate Leader* is to enable you to succeed in your chosen profession by leveraging your previous military training and military experience in ways that create success for your career and improve the skills that you can offer a business. This book will also allow the employers of veterans an improved understanding of how to leverage veteran experience to create a better, more efficient, and more profitable business. Just as in a military operation, in order for the soldier to be successful, the mission must be successful. Veterans need to apply that same logic of advancing their civilian career through successful execution, just as they once did on the battlefield.

Notes

1. Greenberg, Greg A., and Rosenbeck, Robert A., "Are male veterans at greater risk for nonemployment than nonveterans?" *Monthly Labor Review*, United States Department of Labor, Washington, DC, Volume 130, Number 12, December 2007, pages 23–32.

2. Walker, James A., "Employment characteristics of Gulf War-era II veterans in 2006: A visual essay," *Monthly Labor Review*, United States Department of Labor, Washington, DC, Volume 131, Number 5, May 2008, pages 3–13.

SECTION 1

UNDERSTAND

Understanding how you add value to a commercial organization is essential in order to fully leverage the capabilities and qualities that you bring to a business. The Understand section of *Combat Leader to Corporate Leader* seeks to help you understand the perspective of an employer, what the employer requires of you to be successful in the workplace, and how military skill sets can influence a successful corporate career. Your experience, an unwavering ethical foundation, a commitment to excellence, an expanded network of professionals for ideas and contacts, and an understanding of common veteran mistakes all will help you understand the business, company culture, and business interactions, and how you can add value to the organization's success.

CHAPTER 1

VETERAN LESSON 1: VETERANS BUILDING BUSINESSES, EMPLOYEES, AND THEMSELVES FOR COMMERCIAL SUCCESS

In business and the military, the goal of each organization is to win with honor and integrity. A military unit seeks to gain terrain and the good will of the population while minimizing the amount of damage caused, as well as ensuring the lowest number of friendly and enemy casualties, in order to accomplish the mission. The military skill sets, resourcefulness, leadership, and planning abilities that military combat veterans have applied in Iraq, Afghanistan, Somalia, Kuwait, Grenada, Panama, Vietnam, and Korea, can be applied to help businesses and their employees become even more successful.

The Premise of *Combat Leader to Corporate Leader*: Military Training and Experience Create a Knowledge Base for Superior Business Results

The central premise of *Combat Leader to Corporate Leader* is that your military training and experience provide a core foundation to excel in business and promote the overall financial performance of the corporation. The goal of business is to create services and products that customers value and that lead to an above-average rate of return—in other words, a profit—for the company's owners, the shareholders. In the end, this allows the business to sustain its operations profitably, to ensure continuing success. All businesses strive to create a sustainable competitive advantage that will allow them long-term success. However, central to all of these efforts to create a competitive advantage is the role of the company's employees. Finding, hiring, training, and keeping the best employees are absolutely essential steps for a company to remain competitive, profitable, and innovative. You can become a competitive advantage to your business by applying your military training and experience to successful business practices.

The secondary premise of *Combat Leader to Corporate Leader* is this: Veterans and their employers benefit when veterans are properly employed and motivated to utilize all of their skills for the dual good of the employee's career and the company's business success. Today, the largest gap in the existing veteran employment process is that veterans and their employers have not been directly shown a path or methodology describing how veterans' experience and training can best be used to improve company business results. In bare terms, veterans have the skills and motivation to contribute more to the commercial success of a business—they just need a pathway to best utilize those skills. The gap between success in the military and success in the business world is not as great as one might imagine.

Military Veterans Offer the Value and Excellence Companies Need to Succeed

Starting your career outside the military will be an exciting and demanding— but equally stressful—time. This military-to-civilian career transition is marked by competing sources of stress: (1) leaving the military environment behind, and (2) entering the wide field of unknowns reflecting the civilian commercial business. Great companies are based upon a sustainable value proposition of creating and maintaining value for a variety of stakeholders. Customers find the products or services the company produces to be satisfying to meet their needs; stockholders find the return that the company produces to be equal to the comparable risk/reward ratio of other similar ventures; and employees find the time spent at the workplace to be engaging, interesting, and rewarding. When any one of these three elements fails, the company usually does not succeed. The central driver for success in business is the employee. Employees create products, satisfy customer needs, meet financial obligations, and make the critical decisions to guide the company to success. Therefore, finding and keeping the finest employees is the most important decision for a company.

As a veteran, you offer vital real-world experience, critical decision-making skills, unsurpassed integrity, a strong leadership ethic, excellence in execution, and employee coaching and development skills that can make you a vital element in the success of any business. Additionally, due to your core military experience and training, you offer essential skills to lead the firm to greater business success. You have been taught how to create integrated operations plans with multiple contingencies to ensure that critical strategies succeed, how to create and develop personnel to succeed in their careers, and how to coordinate the placement and use of critical resources to ensure that a plan has the best chance of success.

Examples of Veterans in Business and Government Creating Value

The following four examples offer a fantastic representation of the full range of career possibilities that veterans have once they depart military service. In all three of these cases, their military service acted as a springboard for greater career success and satisfaction.

J. Craig Venter, PhD, is an unlikely veteran who made an enormous impact on business, medicine, and the future of healthcare. Venter was a U.S. Navy corpsman from 1967 to 1968 and served in a field hospital in Vietnam treating severely wounded marines, sailors, and soldiers. Following his military service, he earned a PhD in physiology and pharmacology. Following some further medical education and medical research positions, he founded Celera Genomics, which became one of the leading organizations in mapping human and other DNA.

Dawn Halfaker, the chief executive officer of Halfaker and Associates, is a West Point graduate and a combat-wounded veteran. Dawn was a U.S. Army military police officer, gravely wounded in Baghdad, Iraq, in 2004 as the insurgency in Iraq was rapidly gaining strength. Dawn has been featured in an HBO documentary and news articles in *Business Week*, the *New York Times*, and many others. Instead of leveraging a disability for sympathy, Dawn leveraged her military skills by founding a government-services business that specializes in national security issues and is built upon a foundation of veteran employees.

Nate Fick, the chief executive of the Center for New American Security (CNAS) in Washington, DC, is head of a leading organization on contemporary and cutting-edge solutions to the nation's most pressing national security issues. Nate was a Marine Corps officer in Iraq and Afghanistan and authored a book, *One Bullet Away*, on his military and combat experiences. Initially, Nate was one of the early members of CNAS as a policy expert, but then he was selected as the CEO due to his unique combination of military experiences and dual degrees from Harvard. Nate employs Andrew Exum, former U.S. Army Ranger, combat veteran of Iraq and Afghanistan, and author of *This Man's Army: A Soldier's Story from the Frontlines of the War on Terror*. Andrew is one of the leading experts on the counterinsurgency efforts in Afghanistan, Iraq, and Pakistan. Today, due to the efforts of Nate Fick and Andrew Exum, CNAS is one of the leading thought organizations in Washington, DC.

The examples of Craig Venter, Dawn Halfaker, Nate Fick, and Andrew Exum represent the full range of the scientific, business, and governmental contributions veterans can make to society. In all these cases, veterans have leveraged their military experience to make themselves better, more passionate, and more effective corporate leaders. These veterans used their skills in leadership, organization, planning, motivation, management, and teamwork to gain their subsequent career achievements. All these veterans have mastered the ability to make their previous military experience work to support their new careers.

Veterans Must Transition Their Military Skill Sets and Experience from Combat to the Corporation to be Successful in Business

Your transition from the military to civilian life will probably be difficult. The civilian world does not carry the same physical danger risks as military service, but it is even more confusing with its unwritten rules and hierarchies, a seemingly "dog-eat-dog" code of conduct, and an always-gnawing concern about where your next paycheck is coming from. Finally, to top off all these concerns with military transition is the question of future career well-being. A question that will confront you just as it has confronted other combat veterans is, "How do I take the experience of combat, military training, all the joy and pain of the people that I knew in the military, and use these experiences as a way to transform my life and build my career once I have left the service?" You will be faced with productively adapting skill sets from a military culture that emphasizes directness, speed, assertiveness, and violence of action, into a civilian workforce culture that emphasizes team decision making, methodical approaches to problems driven by data analysis, and a more supportive, collaborative environment.

Military Qualities of Excellence to Commercial Qualities of Excellence

In order to be successful in translating military skill sets to commercial skill sets, you must understand what are both the military and the commercial qualities of excellence that each organization expects. Figure 1.1 serves as a framework to help you translate the military qualities of excellence upward through each chapter by leveraging your military skill sets to achieve the commercial qualities of excellence.

Military Qualities of Excellence					
Intelligence	Planning & Preparation	Execution	Team Leadership	Subordinate Development	Technical Skills

Figure 1.1 Military Qualities of Excellence.

The military qualities of excellence form the foundation for the successful execution of military operations. I selected these criteria based upon my military experience, knowledge of U.S. military doctrine, successful military campaigns, and battlefield operational characteristics that are in high demand today in numerous parts of the world. This list is not intended to be all-inclusive, but to highlight the vital characteristics of a sound military operation. A successful military operation is based upon the following qualities:

Intelligence—Intelligence is the understanding and incorporation of all aspects of the battlefield environment from weather, terrain, cultural forces, language, enemy force(s), civilian population, etc., and how the various factors of the battlefield environment will act and react as friendly forces pursue their most likely course of action. The successful incorporation of intelligence into military operations not only describes the enemy and how they will act, but also serves as a prediction of their likely courses of action and their anticipated reactions as the friendly strategy is executed. Good intelligence is not all-knowing. Good intelligence provides an accurate depiction of the enemy, how the factors of the battlefield environment such as the terrain and weather will affect the friendly plan, and the most likely actions the enemy will take or plan to take to achieve their outcome.

Planning and Preparation—Planning and preparation is the art and process of preparing military forces to succeed in combat. Military planning involves the military orders process, which determines objectives, assigns responsibility, and assigns primary and secondary tasks to complete. Preparation for combat operations involves the rigorous training of the military forces involved in both primary tasks, but also secondary tasks that may be required in the event that a contingency plan will need to be executed.

Execution—Execution is the art and process of the successful completion of the military mission and key tasks. Primarily, this is not the rote, stale execution of a laundry list of tasks that will lead to a successful military execution. Good execution of a military plan, leading to a successful conclusion, requires adherence to the plan and, more importantly, good "heads up" awareness and personal initiative to know when to depart from and adapt the plan to ensure that the objectives of the original military plan are achieved. Military members know to keep following a plan until the adherence to the plan will not achieve the expected outcomes. At that point, training, initiative, and personal responsibility take over, as personnel adapt their actions to ensure a successful outcome.

Team Leadership—In the military, a team accomplishes every objective or task of value. Furthermore, the military possess few if any tools to give service members more money, a less dangerous assignment, or some needed time at home with loved ones. For example, during the initial days of Operation Enduring Freedom in Afghanistan, a reconnaissance team spent nearly 2½ times as long conducting observation on a planned parachute drop zone than their mission called for. The team leader, rather than simply pulling off the objective, motivated his men by emphasizing its importance and, using personal example, went on half water and half rations to stretch their meager supplies and ensure that the mission would be a success. This type of team leadership, although extraordinary, is in fact very common throughout all the U.S. armed forces. Teams, when motivated and well led, accomplish amazing things.

Subordinate Development—Another leadership skill that the military does exceptionally well is developing subordinates' skill sets both in soft skills, such as leadership and personal skills, and in hard-skill development, such as advanced job training and additional technical qualifications. The military views subordinate development almost as a chain process, whereby a lower-ranking member is trained, educated, and coached to assume positions of increasingly higher responsibility throughout his or her career. Subordinate development is critical because it is executed from one level to the next and to the next, so all members of the military get this development.

Technical Skills—Technical skills are vital because their mastery is what creates an effective combat fighter. A Marine may have great planning and leadership experience, but unless she can fire her weapon accurately, operate multiple radio systems, and operate counter-improvised explosive device (C-IED) equipment, she may very possibly fail in the successful execution of her military mission.

The Commercial Qualities of Excellence

The commercial qualities of excellence are the primary drivers for what makes a business, of any size or service or product, successful. Businesses have to successfully complete an amazing amount of centralized and simultaneous tasks to be perceived competitive in today's marketplace. Businesses must manage cash flow to ensure they have enough immediate money to pay their bills, pay employees sufficient benefit packages so they remain with the company, operate at the lowest cost and highest service level to meet the most demanding customer, and ensure that all of the company's and their employees' activities are both morally, ethically, legally, and socially sound.

I selected these commercial qualities in a similar fashion to the military qualities of excellence because these reflect timeless commercial values of what makes a company successful over a sustained time. Business excellence, both financial and operational, is a continuous challenge to achieve and to maintain, but the qualities listed in Figure 1.2 help businesses ensure that they consistently meet the demands of the marketplace, shareholders, employees, customers, and other stakeholders.

Commercial Qualities of Excellence					
Strategy	Execution	Financial Results	Service & Quality	Leadership	Consistent Improvement

Figure 1.2 Commercial Qualities of Excellence.

Strategy—Strategy for businesses means setting a path and establishing the conditions for success in a venture or ventures that will (1) satisfy financial returns, (2) be difficult for the competition to emulate quickly, (3) be within the skill sets of the business to execute successfully, and (4) be able to satisfy the customer need for the good or service over a sustained time period. Apple made this type of strategy a success when it transformed itself from a computer company into a personal electronics company. Today, Apple is the standard for personal electronic devices such as phones, music players, and portable media devices. A key element of a success strategy is also knowing when to adapt, change, or abandon a strategy that is no longer working.

Execution—Execution is the successful delivery to the customer of the product or service that fulfills the need for which the customer purchased it. The company must execute literally thousands of tasks before a product or service reaches the customer, from purchasing raw materials to transporting goods to conducting advertising. However, all of the events in executions must be viewed through the prism of customer satisfaction and how the good or service satisfied the need of the customer. For example, if I do anything, from developing, to marketing, to delivering a laundry detergent to customers, and that detergent does not clean clothes or make them smell fresh, then I have ultimately failed, because my execution failed to satisfy the reasons the customer purchased the product.

Financial Results—The achievement of above-average financial returns is the reason that businesses operate. It could be a child's lemonade stand or a multinational, multibillion-dollar conglomerate. However, financial results are not only quarter-to-quarter earnings per share returns. Good financial management and results provide an above-market return to shareholders, but they also ensure a good credit rating for the company, timely payment to suppliers and vendors for materials and services, a relatively low debt level, and solid investment levels to ensure the company's future success at meeting its business objectives in a competitive environment. At times, these goals can be contradictory, but they usually can be achieved.

Service and Quality—Customers will buy new services and products to try them out and see if they work. However, service and quality is what will make customers stay—and attract even more customers. Customers demand good service, both in the purchase of a product and in the after-market support of the product. "What if it breaks? What if I have a question?" Many thoughts and concerns run through the minds of consumers on their way to becoming customers. Service and quality are primary factors that make the restaurant chain McDonalds so successful. McDonalds is legendary for its consistent service, quality of food preparation, rigorous engineering of food development, raw food ingredient purchasing, and in-store customer service. I can go from a McDonalds in Key West, Florida, to Portland, Maine, to Seattle, Washington, to San Diego, California, and have the food taste the same with the same service quality. Service and quality are central indicators of the success of a business.

Leadership—Just like military forces, commercial businesses need leaders who possess high ethical standards, rigorous decision-making skills, an analytical mind that can see the perspective of both the firm and the customer, understanding of how to attract and grow

Combat Leader to Corporate Leader Translates Military Experience to Commercial Success!

Commercial Qualities of Excellence

Strategy	Execution	Financial Results	Service & Quality	Leadership	Consistent Improvement

Career Success Factors

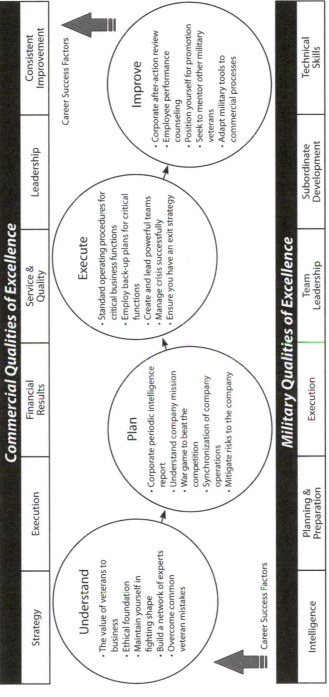

Understand
- The value of veterans to business
- Ethical foundation
- Maintain yourself in fighting shape
- Build a network of experts
- Overcome common veteran mistakes

Plan
- Corporate periodic intelligence report
- Understand company mission
- War game to beat the competition
- Synchronization of company operations
- Mitigate risks to the company

Execute
- Standard operating procedures for critical business functions
- Employ back-up plans for critical functions
- Create and lead powerful teams
- Manage crisis successfully
- Ensure you have an exit strategy

Improve
- Corporate after-action review
- Employee performance counseling
- Position yourself for promotion
- Seek to mentor other military veterans
- Adapt military tools to commercial processes

Career Success Factors

Military Qualities of Excellence

Intelligence	Planning & Preparation	Execution	Team Leadership	Subordinate Development	Technical Skills

Figure 1.3 The *Combat Leader to Corporate Leader* Framework.

talented employees, keen financial sense, and the means to ensure that the company meets all the legal, social, and ethical requirements of its operations. The ethical component is one of the most important qualities for business leaders, because of the positions they hold within an organization and the positive example and tone they set for the rest of the organization. Leaders who meet all of these personal and professional criteria are in short supply in any business, but those who possess these qualities nearly always emerge as the leaders in their companies and underlying divisions. Leaders are the executors of business strategy, and their development must be central to any successful business.

Consistent Improvement—The final quality for commercial excellence is consistent improvement. The modern marketplace—for every business, from a dry cleaning store, to a hot dog stand, to a global corporation—is in a constant state of flux. Customers demand new products, customers want to pay less, governments introduce new regulations, and markets demand ever-better returns. Central to the all of the criteria in the commercial qualities of excellence is the ability to get constantly and consistently better in all of these areas. The process of almost evolutionary adaptation that businesses go through is critical and central to their success.

Improving Veteran Career Success and Making Veteran Employees a Competitive Advantage in Their Companies

The entire focus of this book is how veterans can apply the military qualities of excellence to support and reinforce the commercial qualities of excellence. Simply stated, the purpose of this book is to show former soldiers, sailors, marines, and airmen how to best use their military skill sets and military experiences to succeed and advance in civilian professions. It is not just enough to get a job; the military provides great skills that can lead to fantastic success in the civilian world. While challenge is an inherent part of the transition, it is vital to remember that others have successfully transitioned and succeeded.

This book provides veterans, the employers of veterans, and those desiring the knowledge of veterans, a series of what I call the 20 "veteran points of business value" that can be used to create better business results, and through those business results, help advance your career. These 20 veteran points of business value share a common foundation derived from common military experience and universal military leadership skill sets. The 20 veteran points of business value serve as a bridge from veterans' practical experience and military training to the execution of superior business results. Your progression from a rewarding military career to an equally or more rewarding civilian career is a daunting but far from impossible task that many before you have achieved.

CHAPTER 2

Veteran Lesson 2: Military Ethics and Values Form the Foundation for Business Success

The second lesson is that your battle-tested and enduring sense of values and ethics forms a critical foundation to effective, efficient, and profitable business practices. This strong sense of values and ethics will allow you to add instant value to the company you work for, even though you may have little or no direct experience in the business or industry. This immediate value-add comes from the values and ethics veterans not only firmly hold but also adapt to all of their business practices. Your goal as an employee is to be purpose-driven, ethically based, committed to excellence, able and willing to lead, and committed to operational excellence to satisfy the needs of both the company and the customer. Your value to your employer or potential employer is greater than the "hard" military skill sets of technical expertise. Except in very rare instances, hard skill sets alone are not sufficient for a veteran to adequately relate their skills and experiences, and the value that they bring or will bring to a commercial employer

Military Ethics and Values Shape Business Success

An essential point that many commercial businesses miss, even those who hire veterans, is that the variable conditions of the market, customer demand, and global developments that they find so challenging form a core area of expertise for veterans. Veterans have lived their entire careers in an environment where the only thing predictable is that everything will change, and the mission must still be successful. A firm foundation of values and ethics makes mission success in a shifting landscape possible. What will make you incredibly valuable to an organization is the combination of being an ethical, purpose-driven employee and an employee that can understand, decide, plan, act, and adjust in actions to consistently meet the best interests of the company. Employees such as these are vital to the success of a business.

As a veteran, you received your ethical foundation through training, operational employment, and experiences in the military. The qualities and values a military leader possesses are crucial to the leadership and business environment. People will rarely follow a leader that they do not respect, admire, and wish to emulate. Likewise, customers, investors, and shareholders need to be constantly and consistently assured that they are investing and associating with individuals of value and honor. Before leaders can lead an organization, they have to both understand and possess the values and ethics that will make them successful in the business.

We are in an era of business culture where the images of corporations and their executive positions—CEOs, CFOs, and boards of directors—are more often than not associated with the fraudulent behavior of Bernie Ebers of WorldCom, the self-destruction and deceit of Enron, the lack of ethical accounting oversight at cable giant Adelphia Communications, and the insider trading accusations at businesses too numerous to count. All of these accusations and crimes not only harm shareholder value, but weaken the resolve of workers, drive customers into the waiting arms of the competition, and drive new investors away. The shocking lack of personal ethics of key business leaders has led to the vast majority of business failures in the past few years. Enron is a historical example where personal greed and hubris led to failure to provide proper accounting oversight and endorsed the creation of investment structures whose sole evaluation criteria appeared to be how much of a bonus would be generated for the leaders of the company. Bernie Madoff defrauded thousands of investors and caused the loss of entire fortunes for many through a business practice built upon a nearly lifelong lie. The notion of a company's management being dedicated to the shareholders—the true owners of the company—and using shareholder best-interest to evaluate value creation and risk was completely absent. In these examples and more, the lack of a solid foundation of personal ethics was, in nearly all cases, the most significant contributing factor in the destruction of these companies. In sharp contrast to these executives, every member of the U.S. armed forces began his or her very first day in the military with an oath of professional service that highlights the selfless duties required and a focus on the needs of the country, not the individual. The values and ethics that veterans bring to the work force are invaluable to achieving commercial business success.

Daily, millions of men and women in the armed forces set out to personify a high ethical, moral, and professional standard. In combat, seemingly inconsequential activities, such as vehicle maintenance, security guard duties, and logistical supply duties, take on enormous physical and operational consequences due to the fact that all military activities, no matter how small, lead to the safe, effective, speedy, and successful execution of military operations. The leadership skills that you developed through your intensive training and operational combat experience are well suited for the challenges and operational requirements of the business world. As a military leader, you understood what it was like to operate under high pressure during dynamic, changing situations, and maintain a dual and equally weighted focus on their objectives and on their ethics. Your military leadership skills can be personified by dedication, a winning spirit, thorough planning, and focused ethical action that serve as a guide to provide the values, drive, and spirit to make corporations and businesses succeed. Military values and ethics can be the bridge between building and maintaining dynamic organizations and the quagmire of corporate failures to which too many business leaders fall prey.

Military Leader Ethics and Values

The character of military leader ethics and values is characterized by ten principles. These principles are

(1) Ethics and values
(2) Leadership by example
(3) Leading from the front
(4) Seeing the battlefield
(5) Honesty and integrity
(6) Imagination and anticipation
(7) The will to win
(8) Quality
(9) Winning with humility
(10) Concern for others.

These principles are meant to provide the framework for military leader ethics and values. However, like all frameworks, these principles only provide the bones of the skeleton. It takes caring, decisive decision-making, and a relentless intent to improve, to put the flesh on the bones and make the decisions real.

Ethics and Values

Ethics and values are the foundation of any leader and the decisions that he or she makes. Combat and competitive business both demand an even stronger ethical and value-based form of leadership because these activities are at the cutting edge of the activities of society. Table 2.1 provides some examples of leading with ethics and values.

The situations in which military and corporate leaders find themselves are often intense, heavy with consequences, and time-compressed, and a wrong decision could

Table 2.1 Examples of Military and Corporate Ethics and Values

Military Examples of Ethics and Values	Business Examples of Ethics and Values
Personally reporting to the commander the failure to complete a mission	Maintaining a price with a long-term customer
Personally rebuilding and restoring an innocent bystander's dwelling that was damaged in combat	Helping former employees find employment following a layoff
Taking responsibility for a subordinate's well-intentioned mistake	Taking responsibility for a subordinate's well-intentioned mistake

result in the loss of crucial resources, the loss of vital customers, or other severe financial consequences. Strong ethics and values form the foundation of a leader so, when under pressure, leaders can make the best decision with the time, situation, and information that they have available. Furthermore, the ethical foundation of leaders forms the character of the organization and the business. The best ethical rule is a modification of the Golden Rule: To lead, act, and react to others in the same way that you would want to be led, be acted toward, and be reacted to.

Leadership by Example

Leadership by example is one of the central tenets of any form of leadership, commercial or military. The definition of leadership by example is the continuous, consistent, and thorough action(s) of the leader to provide a positive role model in both word and deed. From war movies, we are conditioned to admire and respect the seasoned leader who, knowing the dangers better than anyone does, always leads his unit from the front—such as Tom Hanks's character in *Saving Private Ryan*. Another glowing example of this is depicted in the movie *We Were Soldiers*, when the newly arrived junior officer temporarily halts his unit's difficult training for a rest and then walks the line, inspecting his soldiers' feet, instead of resting himself. The principle of leadership by example applies in business just as it does in combat. Genuine business leaders are the ones who go and talk to customers about their businesses and how their business can serve the customer better. Those who lead by example in business may be executives who visit the factory floor to understand their business from the perspective of the line worker, or who sit in on a customer call center to better understand the nature of customer complaints. These business leaders are also willing to go in front of senior management and members of the board of directors to pitch new ideas—and then be the first ones to take those new ideas in front of customers. Table 2.2 provides more examples of leading by example.

Leadership by example takes a great deal of energy, time, attention to detail, and, most importantly, plain, old-fashioned guts. In business, as in the military, there is no substitute for immediate, frequent, and direct personal attention from leaders to ensure that the strategy is enacted, and enacted correctly, at the frontline level. Leadership by example compels leaders to act as they want all of their employees to act. Leadership by example is also not reserved for only the highest levels of leaders. Leaders at every level, from the boardroom to the factory floor, have to demonstrate the principles of leadership by example.

Some of the best instances of leadership by example I have witnessed outside of the military are exactly similar to leadership by example in the military. Later in my civilian career, when I was a member of a leadership-development class, I spent several weeks at a manufacturing site just understanding each worker's position and how they all did their jobs, and an enormous amount of time listening to suggestions on how the site could improve operations. You can use leadership by example as one of the first and most direct ways to build your understanding and credibility within an organization. The simple steps of leadership by example allowed me to be successful in both the Army and my corporate career because they simultaneously

Table 2.2 Examples of Military and Corporate Leadership by Example

Military Examples of Leadership by Example	Business Examples of Leadership by Example
Public scheduling of subordinate quarterly counseling sessions	Interviewing a customer on why they moved their business to a competitor
Running physical fitness training with different platoons on rainy days	Answering customer complaint calls in a phone center
Having the battalion commander personally conduct maintenance on his or her vehicle	Calling a customer to announce a price increase or the removal of a critical service, with an explanation

demonstrated a willingness to go the extra mile, a willingness to learn about all parts of the organization, and the desire to learn and to improve the organization.

Leading from the Front

All military personnel understand that followers will do well only what they see their leaders doing well. This is a basic truism of leadership for both the military and the commercial world. Business leaders need to be out front working with customers, suppliers, and their communities. One of the greatest examples I've seen of leading from the front was one of the directors that I worked with who personally sat for half a day with a smaller customer to explain the business's products and services, as well as to work through issues that were preventing the customer from giving us more business. So there I was in a cramped, overheated office with an executive who operated a multibillion-dollar line of business, working with a customer whose business was a few million dollars a year. What I learned from watching this fantastic interaction was that *all* customers are valuable, and that every person in the organization, no matter how high, needs to take every action to ensure that the company will be a success. That is leading from the front. See Table 2.3 for other examples of leading from the front.

Workers want to see business leaders who have gone and talked with customers about their products and services so they can take this additional perspective back

Table 2.3 Examples of Military and Corporate Leadership from the Front

Military Examples of Leadership from the Front	Business Examples of Leadership from the Front
Personally leading a risky or dangerous mission	Allowing a public scorecard to assess the leader's business effectiveness
The leader being the last person to eat	Personal interview and welcoming lunch with all new employees
The company commander performing airborne jumpmaster duties with the newest member of the company	Quarterly updates to keep all employees informed and updated on the business strategy

and improve the business. As a worker, if my boss or my boss's boss is spending that much time with the customer, then I damn well better be spending twice as much time. Likewise, customers want to talk to their service and product providers to share their perspectives and what they like or dislike about the company's products.

These interactions are what demonstrate excellence, commitment, and dedication to the organization. A fantastic technique for leading from the front is the classic "management by walking around." This technique involves getting outside the office, out from behind the desk, and seeing what is going on in the organization while simultaneously communicating the key points of your strategy and vision. When I was a company commander, this meant going on a cold Thursday-afternoon walk through the motor pool to see what was really going on and what the issues really were. Junior non-commissioned officers and junior officers are taught that if you really want to check your perimeter security, then you check it at 4 AM and not at 8 PM. A leader walking regularly through the organization, interested in and compelling excellence, is one of the most motivating things for an organization. Talking with customers, suppliers, and leaders in the community is not something that can be done well from offices or even over the phone. Business leaders need to be physically out front in front of their customers and their employees, executing the things that matter most.

Seeing the Battlefield

A vital attribute for a leader is the ability to realistically envision the battlefield or business competitive environment. This ability to see the battlefield is from the perspective of both the enemy and the friendly military force. For a military leader, this means accurately assessing, visualizing, and evaluating all of the environmental factors—including weather, terrain, enemy, adjacent friendly military units, and how they may affect the planned outcome of the operation. The business leader is responsible for seeing the competitive landscape, developing requirements for customers, and anticipating legislative implications in order to ensure that the business plan succeeds, customers are satisfied, and the business returns profitable results. Table 2.4 provides examples of seeing the battlefield.

Table 2.4 Examples of Military and Corporate Seeing the Battlefield

Military Examples of Seeing the Battlefield	Business Examples of Seeing the Battlefield
Commanders regularly touring the front and holding discussion with all soldiers of units operating in the area	Keeping a scorecard of indicators on the success of the competition, company business plan, and customer criteria
Consistent monitoring or analysis of enemy communication for insight	Regular use of independent or "secret shopper" to get ground truth
Employment of qualitative and quantitative systems to measure progress	Interviews with potential customers and industry leaders to assess the direction of the industry

Business leaders need to be able to realistically see and evaluate their environment. Too often, business leaders deceive themselves and their shareholders that their products are meeting customer expectations or that the skills of the competition are not growing. A realistic perspective on the competitive landscape will allow business leaders the best vantage point to make honest assessments about what matters most to their business.

Honesty and Integrity

Honesty is living up to a standard in both word and deed. Integrity is the open and consistent public display of a standard honestly arrived at. These attributes of honesty and integrity have to be consistently demonstrated in public and in private, and arrive at the same action or conclusion each time in order for the leader to be trusted. Furthermore, when observed over time, actions that demonstrate honesty and integrity have to be similar and consistent. There is nothing more demoralizing to a workforce or customer base than a business leader who makes a decision and then in private, or later, backs out of that commitment or acts in a way that minimizes or mitigates the decision. Table 2.5 provides some examples of acting with honesty and integrity.

I remember a time when, as a special forces captain in Bosnia, I was serving as the battalion logistical officer, charged with all supply, contract, and resource coordination for my unit. I was creating and outlining the final requirements and specifications for a large bid to supply over 30 locations in Bosnia with generators for a two-year period. As I was putting the draft requirements document together, one of the prospective bidders asked to meet with me to clarify some of the various power and maintenance requirements that were going to be part of the contract. In the meeting with me and my contracting non-commissioned officer, it soon became clear that the prospective bidder had other questions. Toward the end of the meeting, the prospective contractor asked how he could help secure the contract for his company. As we explained the contracting process again, he slowly put two stacks of $5,000 on the table and began to describe a series of hotels and restaurants where he had open accounts on the Croatian coast. My contracting officer and I could easily have accepted the bribe and taken the "benefits" offered, and no one would have been the wiser. However, the principles of honesty and integrity drove us both to summarily and harshly reject the bribery

Table 2.5 Examples of Military and Corporate Honesty and Integrity

Military Examples of Honesty and Integrity	Business Examples of Honesty and Integrity
Honest and timely coaching comments to improve performance	Honest and timely coaching comments to improve performance
Reporting "bad news" to the commander fully and immediately	Reporting "bad news" to the boss fully and immediately
Personally delivering "bad news" to a subordinate	Personally delivering "bad news" to a subordinate

attempt. Ethical decision-making must be clear, consistent, and vigorous in order to be believed.

Imagination and Anticipation

The principles of imagination and anticipation may not seem to be military ethical and value principles, but they most surely are. During the Normandy invasion, the Allies' airborne forces were able to help misdirect Nazi German reinforcements through the use of mannequin parachute forces armed with firecrackers and other noisemakers. While deception is a historical principle of military operations, using puppets and other noisemakers to create a successful diversionary mission is certainly a fantastic example of imagination and anticipation helping missions succeed. Imagination is the use of creativity, insight, and initiative to envision, create, and execute other ways, means, and methods to accomplish a task or mission. Anticipation is the use of foresight, planning, and imagination to predict correctly what requirements will or will not be needed in the future to make the mission a success.

Apple Computer presented a great example of corporate imagination through the development of the iPod devices. The iPod is essentially a small, battery-driven hard drive that plays and stores music in a copyright-protected format. As first glance, this seems to be quite simple. However, Apple's consumer electronic market insight, speed to market, marketing prowess, compelling advertising, and reasonable pricing made the iPod an exceptional commercial victory. On the military side, the first days of the U.S. Army's counter-improvised explosive device efforts were exceptionally imaginative as U.S. Army and U.S. Marine Corps units simultaneously sought to improve armor protection, understand and disable bomb-making networks, and use drones and other intelligence devices to rapidly counter the threat.

Anticipation goes hand-in-hand with imagination because in order for a plan to be successfully executed, a leader must know what is going to happen, and not going to happen, two or three steps down the line. During the recent war in Iraq, the U.S. Army and Marines, after a detailed study of combat fatalities during the Korean and

Table 2.6 Examples of Military and Corporate Imagination and Anticipation

Military Examples of Imagination and Anticipation	Business Examples of Imagination and Anticipation
The use of women in a direct combat role to respect Muslim culture during house searches	The use of one product or service in two or more different markets
The creation and successful use of forward surgical teams in Iraq and Afghanistan	Apple creation of the iPod by using a small hard drive as a portable music player
The U.S. military adoption of distance-learning software for teaching languages and other critical skills	The creation of the "air taxi" service by using private jets in a city taxi service and configuration

Vietnam Wars, discovered that the closer to the battlefield casualty trauma surgeons are located, the better the patients' overall chances for survival. Like the Apple example, this appears to be a "no-brainer." However, in order to operate effectively and safely, surgeons need a sterile environment, skilled nurses to assist, breathing machines, portable X-ray machines, and anesthesia supplies and machines. However, the battlefield need, combined with medical expertise in design, logistics, and support, made these forward surgical teams one of the overwhelming successes of the Iraq and Afghanistan conflicts. Imagination and anticipation are essential leadership attributes. Table 2.6 provides other examples of acting with imagination and anticipation.

The Humanistic Will to Win

The humanistic will to win is one of the most compelling attributes of corporate and military leadership. It is the incorporation of the attributes of desire, leadership, planning, and motivation to lead an organization through the trials of execution to the successful completion of a mission, strategy, or task (see Table 2.7). Equally coupled with the focus on winning is the ability to win in a manner that does not destroy the opponent, but acknowledges them and leaves them with their sense of self-worth intact, as well as their ability to cooperate in the future.

The central difference between the humanistic will to win applied for business and the will to win applied in combat follows the principles of basic game theory. In combat, battles and engagements are treated as "single-round" games. A single-round game is when there is only one round of the game, and if a player does not win that round then he or she will not have an opportunity to play or win again. In combat, when a patrol is engaged by small-arms fire in the Korangal Valley in Afghanistan, team leaders or platoon leaders know that they need to bring every resource, weapon, training, and supporting force to bear as quickly and effectively as possible in order to win. If leaders do not do this, then their lives and the lives of their soldiers may be lost. Therefore, single-round games require a ferocious leadership style that is completely unmitigated in pursuit of victory. However, this style in a business-world setting would be completely overblown in its pursuit of a commercial objective.

Game theory applied to the humanistic will to win sees business engagements as multiple-round games in which a leader does not have to win every round, because the leader will have multiple times to play. Indeed, in multiple-round games, the party who continuously wins begins to be viewed with suspicion and rejected by the group. The key focus of a humanistic will to win is that the business leader ensures that, above all, they win in their commercial action and meet the business objectives. However, the level of ferocity is mitigated in the humanistic will to win. Using this style, the goal is to win with class or win while preserving the other party's sense of self-worth, dedication, and engagement. In most business transactions, it is not possible or even desirable to destroy the competition. Additionally, customers closely observe how one competitor treats another. It is essential that the humanistic will to win style is closely adhered to in order to meet commercial business objectives, but still retain a sense of professionalism, style, and humanity.

Table 2.7 Military and Corporate Examples of the Humanistic Will to Win

Military Examples of the Humanistic Will to Win	Business Examples of the Humanistic Will to Win
LTG Ray Ordinero during Operation Iraqi freedom	Steve Jobs during his return to the Apple CEO position and his transformation of the company
BG Roosevelt walking the line along Normandy beach during the June 6, 1944, D-Day invasion	The decision by Johnson & Johnson during the Tylenol poisoning in the 1980s to remove all Tylenol products to restore customer confidence
Gen. Douglas Macarthur during the planning and execution of the Inchon landing	Warren Buffett and the market performance of Berkshire Hathaway Corporation

Quality

Quality is the capability of a task or service to fulfill all of the requirements for which it was designed, in a continuous, consistent, and highly repeatable manner. For example, word processing software may be well-designed and useful. However, unless the software operates in the same fashion every time and allows the flawless execution of critical processes (e.g., saving and retrieving documents), it would be considered to lack in quality.

For combat, quality is important because if a weapon or radio does not function properly or a soldier was trained improperly, then a unit may take unnecessary casualties, and lives will be lost. The initial failures of the M16A1 during the opening stages of the Vietnam Conflict are an excellent example of how combat material that lacks quality destroys morale and damages fighting ability. In the business world, lack of quality is associated with additional costs (products have to be remade or are scrapped), and consumer confidence in the product or service is severely damaged. Brands such as Lexus, Google, Hewlett Packard, Westin, and Rolex are world-recognized leaders in the quality and services they provide to their customers. The reason that these brands and their products and services have

Table 2.8 Military and Corporate Quality Examples

Military Examples of Quality	Business Examples of Quality
The design and functionality of the AK-47 assault rifle	Lexus automobiles
The creation and implementation of the U.S. military medical evacuation system (medevac)	Market performance of Berkshire Hathaway Corporation
The U.S. Marine Corps small arms marksmanship instruction	Design and performance of Samsung personal electronic products

attained legendary status is based almost solely on their consistent ability to deliver a world-class product each time. Quality is the product and service attribute that, once attained, must be justified each time the product is used. For example, all of the Lexus model years that precede and follow a new Lexus automobile must be just as good or better, or the quality of the brand and product begins to be questioned. This and other examples of quality are provided in Table 2.8. In combat, the lack of quality can kill, and in commerce, the lack of quality can put you out of business.

Humility

Second only to the humanistic will to win is the concept of leader humility. A leader shows humility by displaying active listening and a mind open to new ideas, suggestions, recommendations for improvement, and ways to improve the performance of the business when these are presented by employees, customers, industry peers, and the public (see Table 2.9). Humility is not the open abandonment of principles, business strategy, or determination to accomplish a task in an adverse environment. Rather, humility is the open acknowledgement that all people inside and outside of an organization are vital to the success of the business enterprise. The role of active, engaged listening is vital to the quality of humility. If there is not constant, high-quality active listening involved, then any appearance of humility is wasted, because the leader does not truly care about and embrace what the outside parties are saying. The HBO miniseries A Band of Brothers details the experiences and personalities of a company of paratroopers during World War II. In the series, the character of Richard "Dick" Winters is a textbook example of leader humility. In one scene, during the German western offensive of the winter of 1944, which came to be known as the Battle of the Bulge, Winters is pictured walking the line, talking with soldiers, and using their input and recommendations to help make his decisions. Good leaders employ humility because it enables them to fully understand and appreciate their operations while allowing subordinate workers to fully engage and participate with their leaders for the success of the

Table 2.9 Military and Business Examples of Leader Humility

Military Examples of Leader Humility	Business Examples of Leader Humility
The lack of rank insignia for all soldiers during special forces selection training	The CEO of Malden Mills continuing to pay all workers while the factory was being rebuilt after it burned down
The senior military leader always eating last during field training	CEOs who work for $1 a year or take pay cuts during poor business years
A new second lieutenant or ensign asking for performance feedback from her platoon sergeant	CEOs and senior business leaders who take worker shifts over weekends and holidays

organization. On the commercial business side, the former CEO of Southwest Airlines, Herb Kelleher, was famous for working Thanksgiving holidays as a flight attendant, ticket person, and baggage handler, to allow an employee time at home with his or her family.

Leaders' examples of humility flavor and color the entire character of an organization. Every veteran can remember a time when a senior ranking member shared the privations of a difficult situation, listened to a junior ranking military member and solved a problem, or took a subordinate's recommendation for the solution to a problem and implemented it. When I was a second lieutenant with my first platoon, a mortar platoon in Korea, I would regularly take the mortar gunner's exam alongside every member of my platoon. During these exams, even though I had never been to the same mortar gunnery courses, I still tried and did my best to set a positive example for my platoon. This one simple action of taking the mortar gunner's exam demonstrated that I wanted to learn and would perform a task that I was not 100% proficient at, in front of my platoon. Furthermore, this action carried more good will and was an instant morale boost. It allowed all of my soldiers to give me a regular, good-natured ribbing and was a silent enforcer of high standards, as there was never any soldier that scored below me more than once. The mortar platoon set out to ensure that every member would always beat the lieutenant—always!

Concern for Community

The concern for community marks the final quality of a corporate and combat leader. It is a recognition that for business and the national defense, the community is the single most important group—and its well-being the final, most important goal. Concern for the community is best represented when the steps and actions to make the community better are internalized into the DNA of the business or military organization, rather than forced upon it, to try to bring about a series of actions that do not support the true goals of the business and the overall well-being of the community. Some examples of concern for community are listed in Table 2.10.

In the end, a corporate leader or a combat leader's values and ethics are only as good as their implementation, consistency, and steadfastness to maintain a high

Table 2.10 Military and Corporate Examples of Concern for Community

Military Examples of Concern for Community	Business Examples of Concern for Community
U.S. Marine Corps Toys for Tots program	The Special Operations Warrior Foundation program
U.S. Military support of various non-profit programs	Corporate support of the American Red Cross blood donation program
Spontaneous combat unit support of village schools and hospitals to make a local difference	The 1% for the Planet® program to encourage environmental support

standard in both word and action, in public and in private. Corporate leaders need to have a strong values-based foundation, because without that foundation there can be no consistent and true business value creation.

Summary

Today's business leaders are consistently driven to deliver the absolute best business results, no matter the economic environment or business climate. A firm ethical and values-based foundation will make for ethical and superior business results.

CHAPTER 3

VETERAN LESSON 3: MAINTAIN A PERSONAL IMPROVEMENT PLAN

U.S. society as a whole has an exceptionally high level of trust in its military service personnel. Throughout society and over time, the public looks to military service people as possessing a higher ethical and performance standard than the rest of society. This same level of trust does not extend to business leaders. Images of the leaders of the surge in Iraq, General Petraeus and General Ordinerio, and a key figure in the rebuilding of the U.S. Army, General Cody, stand in sharp contrast to former Enron CEO Jeffrey Skilling and former hedge fund manager Bernie Madoff. The reputation of proficient military service means a great deal, and this level of reputation and respect is a significant reason why business leaders look to hire veterans.

This high level of trust and respect can be a significant point of advantage to you in business. Veterans gain an initial high level of trust, respect, and confidence from the rigorous, demanding, stressful, and compelling life that they led in the military. The daily physical training, regularly scheduled military education, self-development programs, and continuous operational deployments garnered military personnel an almost legendary status and a high level of appreciation from the public. However, this initial level of respect from employers and potential employers is just that: initial. As an employee, you must be exceptionally dedicated and rigorous in order for both yourself and other veterans to maintain a highly disciplined and professional level of respect so that you can fully leverage your military background. Professionalism is not just for the military; it applies equally in the business world.

The Veteran Must Have a Personal Improvement Plan for Career Success

The path for veterans to maintain and improve their corporate professional performance is to have a dedicated personal improvement plan that maintains those critical qualities of respect and then uses their military experience as a professional springboard to expand and improve their commercial business skill sets. This personal improvement plan needs to maintain a focus on professional improvement, driven by individual initiative, with an objective to make the veteran a better, more seasoned business professional. The focus on professional performance needs to drive a focus on both external and internal items.

The Veteran's Internal Personal Improvement Plan Items

The internal components of a personal improvement plan all focus on ensuring that the veteran employee has the mental disposition to be open, relaxed, ready, and willing to excel in a position as well as share their areas of expertise with the organization. The internal personal improvement plan items are

(1) Positive, constructive attitude
(2) Cognitive and physical well-being
(3) Continued professional education
(4) Openness to new experiences

Positive, Constructive Attitude

Attitude is one of the most important mental criteria that will make an employee shine in terms of both performance and leadership. Seemingly, a positive attitude is an external display; however, a positive attitude must be generated internally in order for it to be truly and honestly displayed.

You may struggle initially with how to best demonstrate and reflect a positive attitude after your experiences in combat. After all, it can be exceptionally taxing when there are animated discussions concerning PowerPoint font selections after you have been exposed to the dangers of a combat environment. The key to a good attitude, for the military veteran employee, is perspective. Just because your fellow employees have not been to combat, it does not make them bad Americans, fakes, or cowards. It simply means that they have not been to combat and experienced the same things that you have. Additionally, concerning the mundane items that often generate poor attitudes, your co-workers can and probably are as just as frustrated as you are that they have to spend their valuable time with an activity that seemingly produces no corporate value. Your response should not be to chastise employees (e.g., "While we sit here discussing Times New Roman 12, people are dying") or to tell war stories. You must at all times, especially during periods of seemingly commonplace problems, set the example using both leadership by example and taking on a leadership role to help get attitudes and tasks back on track.

Your role is not only to transform your own attitude during periods of frustration, but also to transform the attitudes of your co-workers so the conversation returns to a focus on positive and constructive work. A positive and constructive attitude is a superb personal and team leadership attribute that all veteran employees must strive to attain and maintain. A positive, constructive attitude helps allow all problems to be seen and experienced in their true light. Indeed, a positive attitude helps reveal problems early, because the veteran employee is concerned with making the entire organization better.

Cognitive and Physical Well-Being

Cognitive and physical well-being is the mental and physical state when your mental purpose is aligned with your physical body. The real purpose of cognitive and physical well-being is to ensure that both the mind and the body are able to experience present events, and exist, in the state in which they are both physically located. The goal is for both the mind and body to exist in a relaxed, healthy, pleasant, and aware state.

The ability to achieve a mentally and physically relaxed state is exceedingly difficult for combat veterans—especially for those who have fought in low-intensity conflicts, due to the persistent and unknown threat of enemy activity. Your transition from combat and your immediate return to the civilian world may have been difficult because reactions to seemingly simple events had to be relearned in the context of peacetime. In combat, the mind literally makes the body forget how to relax in order for the body to remain ready at an instant for the prospect of combat. The hyper-vigilance, heightened awareness, and increased stamina that stress provokes in combat are not useful back in the civilian world.

Your challenge as a combat veteran is to learn and to practice ways to decrease your stress levels and improve your ability to successfully and completely relax. Relaxation can be achieved in a variety of ways. Sports, time spent with family, playing with your kids, volunteering, breathing and mental relaxation exercises, positive mental imaging, hobbies that require a complete focus, and fishing are only a few of the ways to constructively relax. Alcohol, sleeping pills, danger-seeking activities to create an adrenaline rush, and the like are not good ways to relax. Relaxation is vital to become and continue to be a successful and productive employee. Re-learning how to relax and consistently practicing relaxation is a key part of the return from combat and the entry into the corporate business world.

Continued Professional Education

The military professional education goal is to teach both a technical or theoretical foundation and a situational awareness for all military positions. Ensuring that service members begin with a strong base of education is a commonality among all of the military services. For new officers and enlisted personnel alike, the initial entry into the military is almost a year or more of basic military and skills training prior to their first operational assignment. The military services strive to provide continuous professional education throughout a service member's career life.

The awareness portion of military education is largely achieved through personal initiative and self-education. The overall goal of awareness education is to keep a dedicated and open eye on the primary issues that effect the successful day-to-day execution of service members' jobs. The overwhelming point is that education does not stop or start in the classroom. Formal education is a supplement to the awareness of the environment that the military strives to promote on a daily basis.

Veterans in business need to use their personal initiative to follow this concept of education for their business career. The formal portion of their business education may involve a four-year undergraduate in business, a two-year graduate degree in business, a two-year undergraduate degree in a more technical business area, or a combination of these degrees with specialization in the liberal arts, social sciences, or the sciences. Additionally, the formal portion need not be completed at one time. For example, if you want to open a small business, you might start with a small "crash course" private program to teach the basics of running a small business. Then, following the writing of the business plan, you may return to a two- or four-year college to take classes on accounting, information technology, marketing, sales, or finance, and use these short bursts of formal education to drive changes or improvement in your business. The key point is not to be entirely focused on the format of an education, but to be focused on what you want and need to know to advance your career in a timely manner.

Modeling after non-veteran peers and superiors in your business can be particularly helpful in deciding what types of education as well as what subjects to pursue in order to have an effective formal business education. For example, when I attended business school for a Master's of Business Administration, I was notoriously short of formal education in the quantitative areas of statistics, finance, and accounting. I remedied this by taking a very heavy quantitative course load, but then did not take as many classes in strategy and leadership, because in those subject areas I could leverage my military experience.

Another key to success in formal education is not to be too concerned with trying to force an enormous formal business education in a short period of time. Business education is best when it is surrounded by business context based upon day-to-day challenges or upcoming projects. When your educational pursuits combine on a daily basis with your workplace challenges, then you have the vital background necessary to take full advantage of your business education. You can use local four- and two-year colleges, combined with remaining GI Bill benefits as well as any available employer-sponsored tuition assistance programs. The guidelines that make formal business education timely, effective, efficient, and cost-effective are a winning combination.

Openness to New Experiences

As a veteran, you may find your entrance into the world of business to be a humbling and often lonely experience. Military personnel are used to a structured environment, clearly delineated responsibilities, positional responsibilities, and a rank structure for assigning responsibilities. In the commercial business world, organizations are often in nearly a semi-permanent state of flux, due to changing market conditions and company product and service offerings. In addition to the state of the commercial organization, you may be very demographically different from your non-veteran employee peers. Veterans are usually older than their business peers by as much as 10 to 15 years, and veterans have years of experiences that many company employees will not understand or will be completely unaware of.

The summation of all of these uncertainties in the marketplace, fluidity of roles in a commercial organization, and differences between the veteran and non-veteran employee peer groups can encourage a status-quo or "pull back" approach by the veteran employee. You might think, "I will pull back and wait until things settle down, become more defined—and then I will get involved." In fact, you should take just the opposite approach. No matter the expressed definition of workplace activity and company roles, you should dive into whatever roles and experiences are offered immediately. On the popular cable television show *Dirty Jobs*, the host Mike Rowe does an excellent job in each show of literally diving into the worst that the week's chosen profession can dish out. He has experienced the worst the week before but, always open to new experiences, he plunges into ice diving, meat packing, or cleaning sewers. A great employee is always open to new experiences.

You will discover that being open, willing, and excited about new experiences and opportunities will set an excellent example for peers and leaders within your company. One of my first job tasks upon returning from Iraq was to interview large numbers of experienced salespeople, looking for ways to improve an existing sales process. So from Iraq, where I was in charge of a large planning staff and working with some of the finest military professionals in the United States and the world, I had to quickly transition into early-morning and late-night interviews of salespeople who were less than excited to speak to me.

But for all employees, challenge is opportunity. I confronted this opportunity by leveraging the frustration that both marketing and sales staff saw in the old sales process, and using it as a springboard to create a new process that would enable both sales and marketing to be satisfied. The primary point of dissatisfaction for both groups actually revolved around communication. The marketing people wanted to be able to track the progress of the sale, and the salespeople wanted to understand early on what marketing wanted to achieve in terms of strategy, price, and sales terms. The revised sales process featured two to three additional meetings between sales and marketing at the beginning of the sales process, in which both groups could discuss and reach agreement on strategy and success measures. The sales force also agreed to use an existing web-based sales tracking tool so that the entire organization could easily review the progress of the sale. This solution was then presented to the chief sales and marketing officers of the division for their review and approval. So a seemingly boring and tiresome process of interviews was transformed into a way for two separate groups to become satisfied with a new process—and a way for me to achieve recognition within the organization.

Veteran External Personal Improvement Plan Items

The external items of your personal improvement plan all focus on conveying to your employer and to the company that you have the physical disposition to be open, relaxed, ready, and willing to excel in a position as well as to share your areas of expertise with the organization. The external personal improvement plan items are as follows:

(1) Personal appearance
(2) Professional decorum
(3) Professional language
(4) Example-setting

Personal Appearance

There are two general rules of thumb for how you should appear at work. The first rule is that you should plan an extensive reconnaissance of your new workplace or interview location to determine dress styles. Prior to an interview or the first day at work, you should go to the office building or job site and observe how people are dressed and have their hair styled. This type of observational reconnaissance of clothing and hairstyles is vital for the veteran employee to be observed as "fitting in" with the organization. You also want to observe how your closest same-gender boss dresses and styles his or her hair.

The second general rule of appearance is that you should dress somewhere between the typical employee at the worksite and the personal appearance of the superior that is one position higher than your boss. Ideally, as the common corporate appearance goes, you want to dress for the position you want and not the position that you have. Hairstyle and facial hair is an important characteristic to pay attention to as well. You may discover that conservative dress and appearance may or may not be the best choice. For example, if you are trying to enter the music industry, then a personal appearance with more colorful, stylish clothing and an innovative hairstyle may be the way to proceed. However, if you are pursuing a career as a personal financial adviser, then a traditional, conservative appearance is the way to proceed.

As a final word of caution, your dress should be age-appropriate and should not be considered too sexy or too disheveled for the workplace. Dress, appearance, and hairstyle are important, from the initial job interview, to day-to-day workplace interaction, to internal interviews for promotion. You want to dress and appear for the position you want to have in the company and ensure that your appearance matches the style of the industry your company is in.

Professional Decorum

How you carry yourself in the workplace, in front of other employees, and in front of superiors is vital for a successful career. Your goal is to portray a confident, consistent, relaxed, engaged, and supportive physical bearing in the workplace. For many veterans, especially those with direct ground combat experience, physical posture and mannerisms that are too overt, controlling, or aggressive can be a hindrance to a successful civilian career. Likewise, a physical bearing that is too relaxed or seemingly uninterested can also be an obstacle. You need to strike the balance between appearing too relaxed and too uptight. An engaged laugh and a good smile will go a long way toward convincing superiors and colleagues that the veteran employee is a productive and engaged member of the team.

You should also take care in the display of military mementos and pictures in your place of work. Banners or old jackets with, for example, the "Bravo Bastards" logo, as well as images of direct ground combat, will present an image of the veteran employee as much too aggressive or as unable to let go of the "good ol' days." Items such as a coffee cup or a single hat are usually OK to display on a desk. Memorabilia such as old name plaques, items that display your former rank, or departing medal racks should be strictly avoided. You must publicly display the professional workplace image that your new or current employer is looking for.

Professional Language

Your choice of language and tone is vital to your success in business. The language that you used in combat, the barracks, and the field may or may not be appropriate to the civilian workplace. As a general rule, swearing, derogatory comments, crude humor, character attacks, and comments that may reflect a poor or indifferent attitude are absolutely forbidden. Your quality of speech needs to be clear, understandable, free of non-industry jargon, confident, and compelling. Swearing and derogatory comments, even if they are humorous and timely, will not be looked at in a positive light, especially when used among new employees. Over time, once you are known to and know your workplace colleagues, swearing and humorous comments in moderation may be used to project a more relaxed and confident attitude, depending upon the company environment. Finally, any comments that are negative or that can be perceived as negative on areas such as race, people's personal appearance, superiors' performance, others' sexual orientation, other people's significant others, and the like, must be strictly forbidden. Depending on company policy, negative comments in e-mail, voice mail, or phone conversations are usually not considered private and could result in punishment, demotion, or in severe cases, dismissal. Your language must always be clear, concise, confident, and supportive, to portray the best attitude and example possible.

Example-Setting

Once again, as in the military, a positive external example is a great motivator and career builder for veteran employees. An employee who projects a positive and supportive internal attitude and a positive external appearance is a tremendous asset to an organization.

You must have the correct and balanced mix of internal and external employment attributes that fully and consistently demonstrate that you are able to leverage your military past and experience for a successful outcome today. An employee who creates and executes a personal improvement plan for both internal and external attributes to be a better corporate employee will immediately be seen as an asset to his or her organization. Military veteran employees who are unable to transition from their previous military career, and the norms of behavior of their military career, will be a disappointment to their employers and their non-veteran colleagues.

Summary

The challenge to be a good businessperson is exceptional, and a steadfast personal improvement plan needs to be a core part of your new profession. In the military, routine personal professional development was a central and important part of the military profession of arms. Personal professional development remains a core part of being a good businessperson.

Unlike the military, in civilian life you may not find a consistent message of personal improvement from business leaders. Even though there is not always a clear message from senior business leaders, there is a clear, constant, and consistent expectation that all businesspeople will seek to improve themselves. Veterans must use a high degree of personal discipline and personal initiative to become business leaders who are constantly improving. Improving oneself for business means more than just taking classes and continuing to present an external appearance of good grooming and confidence. The creation of a confident and peaceful inner self for the veteran is vitally important. You will have no greater source of strength than appearing relaxed, confident, and ready for challenges at the workplace.

CHAPTER 4

VETERAN LESSON 4:
BUILD NETWORKS OF EXPERTS

All military organizations realize the value that comes from the use of well-connected networks of individuals and groups that can provide key insights into how well a military operation is progressing toward its stated goal. A well-positioned and reliable source can be the deciding point between success and failure in an operation. In late 2003, U.S. and coalition military forces were on a widespread hunt to locate and to capture the former dictator of Iraq, Saddam Hussein. Several months of unsuccessful operations had not yet produced Hussein, and the U.S. military was becoming increasingly anxious for a victory. However, a seemingly unrelated intelligence tip from a low-level source led to Hussein's capture in a matter of hours.[1] Information from a variety of sources, when properly used, can yield incredible results. There are several steps from the military networking process that can be employed to aid in the successful execution of commercial operations.

Networking in the civilian business world should not be confused with spying or other types of human intelligence-gathering activities. Networking is the open and public discussion between a person who has knowledge of a particular subject and a person who wants to know about that subject. Networking is not to be confused with military human intelligence (HUMINT), which is the systematic gathering, collection, assessment, and utilization of conversations. The use of seemingly innocuous business tips was what led to the downfall of several characters in the movie *Wall Street* for insider trading violations. In *Wall Street*, one of the characters uses information from a private conversation for a series of rewarding, but ultimately self-destructive, illegal insider trades—a violation of U.S. Securities and Exchange Commission laws. Your role is to place the use of networks of experts in a true, open, and ethical light, and to be able to derive the best use of the information provided to determine the likely actions of customers, the market, and competitors.

The Value Professional Networking Can Provide

The open, ethical, legal, and systematic use of a series of simple questions to key business contacts on market-related items that leads to answers of strategic business questions is the purpose of using a network of professional contacts. As noted in the later chapter concerning the corporate periodic intelligence report, the "news

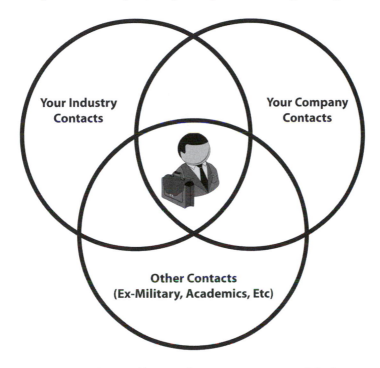

Networking Aligns the Resources of Other Experts to Create a Focal Point On Your Success

Figure 4.1 The Veteran Value of Networking.

test" standard for ethical conduct and corporate responsibility must be rigorously enforced in order to ensure that the interests of the corporation are protected, no one is embarrassed, and the information is gathered in a legal, ethical, and straightforward way, so that everyone in the organization benefits.

As shown in Figure 4.1, networks of experts may be used for more than finding out information outside the walls of the company. Internal networks provide the veteran employee with a support structure, an avenue for mentor relationships, knowledge of new business and professional opportunities, the ability to set up a peer-to-peer network, and the ability to identify and interact with experts who may be required for special projects or daily business questions. For example, personal contacts inside a company's accounting department can be enormously valuable to a marketing professional, because they can yield an improved and more detailed understanding of the company's products and services costs. Finally, internal networks are often self-supporting, with favors traded back and forth that yield incredible results. For example, you may want to spend time with field maintenance personnel, teaching them about leadership and project planning. The return comes when those field maintenance personnel relay back financial opportunities that they may discover after visits with customers. In the end, these relationships are mutually supporting for the employees and mutually beneficial for the company's business success.

Corporate networking processes may also be used to gain knowledge of industry trends, customer insights, and emerging technology. The veteran in a commercial organization needs to have a vast array of contacts inside and outside the company, in various industries, and in academic departments. These contacts can provide the veteran with competitor information, deeper insight into how customers see the company's products, concepts for future products, and trends in their own industry and others that may point to a shift in the overall nature of the business.

One of the best uses of networking is to discover new trends within an industry of customer groups, to help determine the strategic direction the company should take. For example, while a veteran is attending a technology conference, she may seek out suppliers of component parts for laptop computers to help determine whether they see their costs rising, the stability of commodity prices, or how transportation costs may be influencing their bottom line. The goal of networking is to use company internal and external sources to efficiently and thoroughly discover the major "unwritten" trends and insights within an industry.

Networking Steps: Create a Network Successfully

While at face value networking appears to be a simple process, it can actually be quite complicated to determine who the internal and external experts are, to set meetings, and to follow up so you can build a relationship. In networking, the actual meeting and discussion with the identified expert is the easiest step; veteran employees need to conduct extensive pre-work to make sure that the networking session yields the best possible use of their time and gets them the answers they seek. There are five steps to conducting a networking session:

Networking Step 1: Determining What You Want to Know or Accomplish

Networking Step 2: Determining Whom to Contact

Networking Step 3: Background Research for the Networking Session

Networking Step 4: Conducting the Networking Session

Networking Step 5: Following Up after the Networking Session

By following these five steps, the veteran employee will create a strong network of what they want to know, identify the individuals who know the information, and gain the necessary background knowledge to have an intelligent discussion of the issues. In addition to increased knowledge of the company and the industry, networking builds strong contacts and relationships for job searches and other employment opportunities.

Networking Step 1: Determining What You Want to Know or Accomplish

You should always have a clear objective in mind for your session—know what you want to accomplish. The best idea when networking is to have a plan ahead of time about what you want to know, but not necessarily have specific questions memorized. Networking is best accomplished by employing question themes that you want to know and then allowing the conversation to flow around those questions. The background research should be used as a guide to understand what the company is doing, has done, and is trying to do. You should limit yourself to two to three major questions for a networking session. Any more questions or topic and you may not have time to discuss them within the allotted period. In addition, by limiting your questions, you leave some room to pursue additional information and lines of questions.

You should be very cautious and aware when designing your questions and themes to discuss in your networking meeting, to ensure that they are not unethical and do not place your networking contact in a bad position. For example, if you were meeting with a supplier, you would not want to ask questions such as what his private prices to his customers are, who his top customers are, and when his next contracts are due for renegotiation. In this example, your conversation with the supplier should revolve more around what are the most important product design points for his customers, what trends he sees in the industry, or a discussion of some important piece of business news. These strategic discussion questions, as opposed to simple, tactical business questions, will help lead your company to greater strategic insight, especially when the same questions are asked of a larger group of individuals.

The questions to the contact should be outside what is available in normal media channels, to best utilize their time and experience. For example, a discussion on a business topic that was well and thoroughly reported in a local newspaper is not the best topic to discuss directly with a networking contact. The local newspaper article can be used to discuss background on another topic or as an opening for a related issue. The central point is that the purpose of a networking meeting is to gather information that is important to the company strategy but that has not been completely covered in another media source.

Networking Step 2: Determining Whom to Contact

Once you have determined what you need to know, then you proceed with finding out whom to contact for the information. Networking is best done by casting a wide net around various company, customer, industry, and academic professionals. You do not always need to speak to a lone industry or customer expert to find out information that is extremely relevant and vital to your company's operations and success.

The best way to determine a potential networking contact is to look for a primary contact who is an expert in the area that you want to learn more about, and then find two or three people who work for or with the primary subject matter expert. Approach these two or three individuals systematically to see whether each of them will meet with you for a networking session. For the initial and subsequent meetings, it is always best to describe why you want to meet and what the topic of discussion will be. If any of these people cannot meet, you should always ask for two to three additional names of people who are experts in the area, and their contact information. In this way, you can quickly grow a network of contacts. For example:

One initial contact provides

Three additional contacts, who provide

Two additional contacts each, which equals

Ten total contacts.

You can also leverage your position as a veteran to help seek a connection with any variety of contacts. For example, you can use keyword searches of company or industry biographies on popular Internet search engines to look for company executives who have had military experience. Additionally, you can ask to meet with employees of the company who are members of the Guard or Reserve and just recently returned from deployment. You should also look at other points of commonality, to leverage your background with a potential networking contact in order to spark interest and a reaction. The use of hometowns, common educational institutions, military branches of service, common military schools attended, or participation in the same operational campaigns are all very good examples to use for creating a sense of commonality between two strangers.

Networking Step 3: Background Research for the Networking Session

The networking session also requires advanced preparation to understand all of the current issues, challenges, and successes that the business and the person you are networking with are experiencing. It is potentially damaging to a networking session when the person you are talking to has to explain their business model, who their primary customers are, what recent public challenges have occurred in the business, and the recent successes of the business. In the late 1990s in Bosnia-Herzegovina, as part of the NATO-led Stabilization Force under Operation Joint Forge, U.S. military special operations forces served as joint commission observers (JCOs) to help support the successful implementation of the Dayton Peace Accords.[2] The role of the JCO was to act as an impartial observer and communicate the perspective concerning the progress and pitfalls of the peacekeeping mission to the NATO and other multinational division commanders. A central point of the JCOs being able to accomplish their mission of conversation with local leaders was preparation. Prior to a meeting, the JCOs would review translations of local papers, notes from previous meetings, transcripts from local TV reports, and U.S. national media reports on Bosnia. The payoff from this detailed research was instant rapport with the mayors, chiefs of police, politicians, or businesspersons that the JCOs were speaking with that day. Background preparation is vital to ensure a successful networking meeting.

As a general guide, for every 30 minutes of conversation, you should plan 60 minutes of research on the company and the individual. Your research on the company or organization that your networking contact works for should focus on the products and services they provide, who their primary customers are, their recent successes and failures in the marketplace, and what they are doing to combat trends within their competition and the industry. Statistics such as revenue, profit margins, etc., are helpful to know in relative terms, but one does not need to be able to completely recite a company's financial statement. Quotes from key company leaders or primary customers are always good to have available, since these often yield key insights into the company.

There are varieties of websites and news organizations that provide good financial and business news. Here is a brief list of some of the most valuable websites for information sources. This list is not intended to be comprehensive, but is for illustration purposes only.

Websites for Information-Gathering for Networking Sessions

General Internet Search	Google.com, Bing.com, Ask.com
Business Search	Google Business, Yahoo Finance, CNN Money
Major Business Newspapers	*New York Times, Wall Street Journal, Financial Times*
Private Periodical Search	Lexis-Nexis, Ebsco, Factiva
Macroeconomic Conditions	Bureau of Labor Statistics (BLS), U.S. Dep't of Labor Individual Company's Products,
Services, Investor Information	Company-Specific Website
Investor Websites	Fidelity, Vanguard, USAA, E*Trade

Networking Step 4: Conducting the Networking Session

The actual start of the networking session should be kept as simple as possible and should be a part of a regular meeting or previously scheduled meeting. The first item of concern is the time and location. The best networking occurs when both you and the person you are networking with are removed from your daily settings and are not under severe time pressures. When conducting a networking session, it is often difficult to capture the full and undivided attention of your conversation partner because they are distracted with their e-mail, phone calls, customer-problem calls, and the like. Settings such as restaurants, coffee shops, or outdoor malls work exceptionally well because they are often located close to businesses, they may be inexpensive, and they are a public setting that provides a quick getaway from an office environment. If you are working with a person who has a deadline, a family crisis, or some other pending obligation, then it is best to reschedule or temporarily postpone the networking session until both of you can give your undivided attention.

The time of day for the networking session is the next important component. The best times are usually the middle of the morning to the middle of the afternoon, including the lunch hour. Too early in the morning, and your partner may have daily obligations such as a scheduled fitness appointment, day care drop-off, and the like. Likewise, evening times are often more hectic due to rush hour, getting children to evening activities, day care pick-ups, or finishing last-minute work activities. The time of the week is another important component. Monday and Friday should be the choices of last resort, since these days involve, respectively, preparing and completing the week's work. For businesspeople who travel, Tuesday and Thursday may be travel days, but if you can arrange to meet someone at the airport or during a long layover, that can be a great way to transform an otherwise boring travel day into a great opportunity. The length of the session should be relatively brief, around 30–60 minutes, to allow time to have a brief meet-and-greet, and then be able to ask a few questions and discuss the implications.

The conclusion of the networking session must have a recap of the major issues discussed, a few minutes to re-confirm the next steps that both parties will take and when they need to be accomplished, and the date, time, and location of the next meeting. The networking session should always end on a positive note to recap successes as well as confirm what needs to be done. Again, you should always ask to get two to three other names of relevant individuals so that you can expand your contact list.

Networking Step 5: Following Up after the Networking Session

A great step following a networking session is to write a quick note card and mail it to your networking contact immediately following the session. Today, with e-mail, very few people receive any type of personal physical correspondence. This lends an air of instant credibility to a mailed thank-you note, because it grabs and focuses the contact's attention. A nice touch with either a physical letter or an e-mail is to send along a recent article (published within the past seven days) that provides more background on an issue of discussion in the interview. This way, you return the time of the networking session with an educational article that helps your networking contact stay on top of his or her game.

You should also record your networking contact's address, phone, e-mail, likes, dislikes, any next steps that you need to do, the date of your meeting, and any future dates for follow-up activity. Also, record the answers to your business questions so that you can easily compare the answers to each question from your full portfolio of networking contacts. The networking session is to help gather key business information and trends, so you need to take deliberate steps to record and safeguard this information for future use. Spreadsheet and database programs offer easy-to-use and powerful functionality to record the results of these meetings.

Networking Note 1: Using the Networking Session for Employment Opportunities

The purpose of a networking session for employment is to establish a connection or as many leads as possible to people who will be connections in the hiring process. Ideally, networking sessions for employment are conducted with people who have as much influence as possible in the hiring process. If the networking contact is not directly in the line of responsibility for making a hiring decision, then the contact should be used to help identify actual and potential job opportunities, how the veteran job candidate's skills best fill strategic gaps in the company's skills, and the personalities of the hiring managers. At all times, despite the level of the contact, you must ensure that you have a cover letter and resume available to share with your networking contact. Additionally, professional dress, language, and decorum are necessary because networking contacts will be placing their reputations on the line if they recommend the veteran job candidate for an interview. No matter these contacts' level in the organization, the veteran job candidate must treat them with an exceptionally high level of respect and decorum.

This type of networking session must focus on the mechanics of the open position(s), such as job responsibilities, hiring dates, and the interview team for the position. The goal for the veteran job candidate will be to convince the individuals in the networking discussion that you are capable of doing the open job(s) exceptionally well, that you will fit into the culture and skill sets of the organization, and that you will be able to advance within the organization. As a candidate, you will want to show you motivation for an open position, but above all else, you want to completely demonstrate that you are the best choice of an interview candidate for a position.

The best outcome for a series of networking sessions for a military job candidate is an interview. The networking session is meant to "humanize" and more fully expand a veteran job candidate so you can more readily compete against the full pool of candidates. However, networking sessions will not gain a person employment. A well-researched, planned, and executed networking session will ensure a strong look and, in the best cases, an interview.

Networking Note 2: Potential Ethical Minefields in Networking

The appearance of all networking meetings and conversations must always meet the full ethical and legal obligations of your business. First, you should never network with direct competitors, no matter how innocent the reasons or motivations. The appearance of two direct competitors in a closed-door discussion brings many potential legal implications for both companies, and the appearance of two competitors meeting makes for an incredibly bad appearance in front of existing and future customers. Second, you should also be mindful of any potential meetings that may appear to be improper to the casual observer. For example, for a male and female meeting, there should be caution against meeting late in the day or in a remote, private setting. These types of meetings are best arranged for open, public locations, so there is no potential for the meeting to be interpreted as an improper liaison. Furthermore, this avoids the potential of an appearance of ethical miscon-duct for both parties. Appearance matters in all things, especially business.

Third, in your discussions with customers, industry representatives, and others, you must strictly avoid any quid-pro-quo discussions using open or closed language. A quid pro quo is when information or something of value is offered in return for something of equal or greater value between the two parties. Specifically, if a customer offers you a competitor's price sheet or a private example of a product and then asks for a discount or a series of discounts, you need to be prepared not to take any of the items, immediately end the meeting, and notify your superior(s) and your company's legal counsel. Networking discussions are very different from corporate espionage, and the veteran employee needs to be acutely aware of the pitfalls.

Fourth and finally, if something feels bad for you in a networking session, then the best course of action is to stop, regroup, and discuss the incident with a trusted advisor. For example, during a networking session with a customer, the customer may "accidentally" place important papers or competitor contracts on his or her desk for you to see. In this case, the Golden Rule of "Do unto others as you would have them do unto you" works well. It is better to graciously end the meeting than to be accused by your competition of using anticompetitive tactics to sell your business.

Summary

Networking is a business tool of exceptional value to keep a close eye on the trends of the industry, in order to help lead your company to success. However, the pitfalls of networking incorrectly must be always in the forefront of your mind so that you can represent yourself and your company in a manner that is publicly open and highly ethical, and that will successfully deflect any temptations or alleged improprieties. Networking helps your company gain information that it would not otherwise have and then use the information to help compete more effectively, while simultaneously maintaining a very strong ethical and moral standing.

Notes

1. Garamone, Jim, "4th Infantry Captures Saddam near Tikrit," American Forces Press Service dated December 14, 2003, on http://www.defendamerica.mil/articles/dec2003/a121403b.html accessed on 5/25/2009.

2. Baumann, Robert F.; Gawrych, George W.; and Kretchik, Walter E., Armed Peacekeepers in Bosnia, Fort Leavenworth, KS, Combat Studies Institute Press, 2004, pages 203–208.

CHAPTER 5

VETERAN LESSON 5: OVERCOME COMMON MISTAKES VETERANS MAKE IN THE WORKPLACE

Military experience can transform your second career into a success. However, if you cling too tightly and too rigidly to your past military experience, then your career can slow or derail. Veterans can make a number of mistakes if they apply their previous military experience and training to their new employment situation without modification. There is a common misperception among some veterans that the same actions and qualities that made them successful in the military will make them successful in the business world. Veterans entering the business world need to employ their military experiences and training as a leverage point to bring greater career success—and not have their military experience be an anchor to their success in a new organization.

Mistake 1: Leaning on the Past and Not Pushing toward the Future

A strong tendency among all veterans once they are removed from their military experiences is a reversion to their former military way of life in smaller shapes and forms. For example, you may spend an increasing amount of time trying to keep in touch with an old network of military comrades, or you may spend time putting a Class A dress uniform in inspection order or making sure that all your military records are perfect. In extreme cases, some veterans may wear all or parts of their uniform around the house in an attempt to recapture that sense of belonging and order they had while members of the military. In small amounts, none of these things is particularly bad, and they may even be helpful in aiding the veteran in a more successful transition from the military to the corporate world.

You need to spend your time looking forward to the new challenges in your career and life. Your challenge is to fully leverage your military experience and training to help solve the company's business challenges. You do not want to be in a position, or be placed in a position, where you base all of your self-worth and employment value on what you did in the past. True to form, your best day needs to be today and not yesterday. Also, just as in the military, you will have to work long, difficult, and constructive hours to become, maintain, and improve yourself as a world-class professional employee. The original and continuing challenge for veterans is that they must constantly view their military experience as a springboard to improve their corporate performance.

Mistake 2: Treating Others Based upon Your Past Rank and Position

No employee will ever forget the first time they hear a veteran state, "*Well, we used to do it this way in the [State Your Service].*" The employers of veterans and the communities in which they live sincerely appreciate and value the experience and combat service that veterans have performed in the defense of their country. However, the value that an employer expresses in support of military service does not translate into a blind obedience to accept veterans into their workforce without vetting or to adopt 100% the military solution as the best solution to their commercial problems. You must use your past military experience as a point of advantage to make yourself a better commercial employee and not use your military experience as a "hammer" to bring everyone in line with your way of thinking.

You may experience joining the civilian workforce as if you were becoming a private all over again. There are new faces, new positions, open and silent rank structures, a new social structure, tasks to learn, business models to understand, and operations procedures to embrace. One of the central points of disconnect is that a veteran is viewed as a brand-new member of the organization, a private. However, you will see yourself as highly experienced. You'll remember how it was before, to be treated with respect and deference because of your rank, the badges on your uniform, and your former mission focus on immediate life-and-death responsibilities.

Even if you were a junior military member, you could still be hampered in your future commercial service by how you were treated on active duty. Many junior military members were used to being given orders, not encouraged by their superiors to take the initiative to solve problems or to aggressively, but respectfully, disagree with superiors. Junior service members may need to become more vocal and outspoken in their recommendations for solutions, and embrace a more far-reaching leadership style.

The challenge for veterans of all ranks is to maintain their military bearing, military presence, and military trust in an open and non-aggressive manner to convince people that they are ready, willing, and able to learn and contribute to solve today's business challenges. As a new employee, you must re-prove yourself in the trenches of corporate America while retaining all of your previous military background, skills, and trust. Once you have mastered the business skills and military skills applied to business, you can fully capture the trust and confidence of your new employer and fellow employees.

Mistake 3: Not Adjusting Military Presentation, Bearing, and Speech Style to the Corporate World

Military personnel are great presenters, but usually only to a military audience. Military personnel pitch presentations well because they are confident, succinct, direct, aggressive, and passionate. All of these qualities make a great presenter, but the direct and aggressive style of military presentations can at times not be the best style for a corporate environment. The military essentially teaches and enforces a singular presentation style that has the speaker on her feet, in front of a group of high-ranking officers seated in the first row, with a very detailed agenda to direct the entire presentation. The military presentation style is a great example of the "telling" presentation style, where a directed information exchange is the primary goal.

The corporate style of presentations employs a "selling" style. The selling style of corporate presentations seeks to inform the audience and senior leaders just as a military presentation does. The primary differences between the "telling" and "selling" styles of presentations are the audience focus and delivery style. Using the "selling" style of corporate presentations, the focus becomes a much softer approach to the ideas and concepts of the presentation, which seeks to convince and entice to a decision, as opposed to a very direct and forceful sell. The purpose of both the military and corporate presentation styles is the same—to have your idea approved and accepted. The difference is that in the corporate style, you want to create allies who will help you successfully execute your new idea.

In the "selling" presentation style, the first area of focus is the audience. The organizational hierarchy of most corporations in the United States does not follow the strict top-to-bottom rank structure that the military does. Most times, a person will have, at a minimum, two or three different bosses to report to and to take instruction from. Further complicating the already-complex hierarchies of corporations is the fact that peer leadership is exceptionally important to accomplish anything. Peer leadership is the employment of a leadership style of networking, favors, leadership by example, information sharing, and skill-set swapping between employees in a corporation who are at the same or lower positional grade levels in the corporation. For example, in order to successfully complete a new product introduction, a salesperson will have to work with peers in accounting, marketing, operations, engineering, customer service, and transportation, to name only a few. In all of these cases, the salesperson will have no positional authority over any of these people. This calls for the strong and frequent use of peer leadership in order to accomplish the task successfully. The audience focus of presentations is vital. You may be presenting to the vice president of a corporate division, but your presentation will also be strongly focused on convincing your peers that this project makes sense, that their participation will be vital to the project's success, and that they will be recognized for their efforts. The audience is more than the corporate superior in charge of the project. You also have to convince everyone whose help you need to make the project successful, to give his or her full effort and corporation.

The second area of focus in the "selling" presentation style is a modification of the delivery style. The "selling" delivery style is composed of three elements: (1) a relaxed and confident presentation style; (2) the use of data to support major elements of your argument; and (3) a very strong focus on pre-selling and negotiating the recommendations of any presentation prior to its delivery. The greatest problem with a direct translation of the military presentation style to the corporate business world is a problem with credibility. A strong presentation style can look too forced, so that the strength of the presentation style detracts from the credibility of the argument's presentation. The best presentation style comes across as relaxed and confident. A relaxed and confident presentation style positions the presenter as prepared, open to discussion, able to succinctly handle a discussion, and able to bring the group around to his or her perspective and decision. A word of caution: a relaxed presentation style is not sloppy, unprepared, or disrespectful of dissenting opinions. When a presentation or a business decision is prepared using a respectful focus on the audience, supported by multiple data points, a presentation atmosphere that encourages discussion, and an environment that reaches a decision, then a relaxed and confident presentation style is achieved.

The presenter should also have multiple points of data from multiple sources to support his or her arguments, observations, and recommendations in a presentation. The author of the presentation can use statistics, customer quotes, observations from the media, government and academic studies, and survey data to convey the support for or against a business argument. However, an overload and a flurry of statistics does not prove a business argument. Statistics are best employed in a consistent and methodical manner to represent the best decision for the company's business strategy. The following list shows an example of a presentation format to identify and solve a business problem using supporting data.

Presentation Outline for Business Problem and Recommended Solution

(1) Market and customer conditions, with supporting data.
(2) Current company business conditions and results, with supporting data.
(3) Relevant trends in the industry.
(4) Statement of the business problem.
(5) Success criteria or indicators required to solve and/or show progress toward the resolution of the business problem.
(6) Possible courses of action to solve the business problem.
(7) Recommendation of which course of action to use to solve the business problem.
(8) Opinions on the recommended solution by key business leaders involved in the execution of the solution.
(9) Outstanding risks or other items not solved by the business solution.
(10) Additional resources required to make the plan a success.
(11) Senior management decision slide; restatement of the business problem and the proposed solution.
(12) Timeline and next steps for business solution implementation.
(13) Questions and discussion.

This format guarantees that the presentation will follow a logical, data-supported progression from evidence through options to a business solution. This format may be modified, with items added or removed, but the overall flow of the presentation should contain, at a minimum, a description of the environment, a statement of the business problem, the use of metrics to describe the business's current state and results, and an explanation of how the recommended solution will improve the business operations. Including these items as a minimum will ensure a thorough and well-described business presentation.

The final step before any major presentation or business solution is to pre-sell the business presentation and any recommended solutions to the entire team. This is done for two primary purposes. The first purpose of the presentation pre-sell is to allow a period of criticism, review, and input from other business team leaders and experts to provide their insights, opinion, data, and recommendations for the solution. The second purpose of the presentation pre-sell is to reach a consensus on any arguments or points of differentiation on the solution. If no consensus can be reached, then the disagreement can be raised at the meeting so a solution can be crafted. This use of pre-selling the presentation contents and results is a critical component to "selling" the presentation to the team. The ability to present in a well-organized, passionate, clear, and succinct manner, using a presentation format that describes the environment, the problem, and how the solution will improve the business results, is vital. Military members who use the "telling" form of presentations will not build the background consensus for their solution, nor will they fully engage as members of the team as they will by using the "selling" presentation style.

Mistake 4: Letting Yourself Get Too Far Away from Military Appearance, Grooming, and Fitness Standards

Veterans from every service carry a strong, unspoken, and increasingly relevant expectation to "look the part" of a member of the military, even if they are no longer on active duty. The public and corporate America's expectation of higher standards of appearance for veterans is in large part created and exacerbated by the relatively small numbers of recent veterans in society today. In the United States today, veterans comprise only about 1.6% of the U.S. population. Therefore, there is a realistic expectation that in a workplace, there will be at best a handful of fellow workers who know a veteran at all—and an even smaller number who know a recent veteran of the Iraq and Afghanistan wars. The vast majority of the U.S. population and U.S. business world gets their information on military members and veterans from recruiting commercials, the media, and the movies. The overwhelming media message about veterans is positive, so there is a strong perception among the population at large that veterans are a group of capable, hard-working, experienced, and tested group of individuals. With this initial positive perception, the proper physical appearance becomes even more important in order for veterans to meet and exceed public expectations.

Naturally, there is a commonsense structure to the public expectation of a veteran's appearance. A veteran is expected to appear clean-cut, close-shaven, fit, well groomed, and conservatively dressed. This applies equally and fully to both men and women. This does not mean that the public expects or demands that a veteran look just like a member of the active military. Indeed, hairstyles that are not common in the civilian world, such as the military "high and tight" haircut, will look awkward and out of place. But equally out of place are hairstyles that are too long, unkempt hair, or beards of excessive length; these do not meet the common public perception and image of a veteran.

Fitness and dress are further areas of concern for the veteran employee. Veterans are not expected to be at the same high levels of physical fitness that they were in while on active military duty, but their appearance is expected to be neat, not sloppy or disheveled. A neat appearance can also be well accomplished through neat, conservative dress—even of inexpensive clothes. Simple, classic business-casual clothes, consisting of dress pants, a long-sleeved button-down shirt, a jacket, and a tie (if appropriate) is a winning combination for men. For women, dress slacks paired with a jacket or a conservative dress are an excellent, professional business ensemble for nearly any occasion. You will need to spend a few hundred dollars on business clothing—not thousands. Conservative traditional dress is preferred over the latest fashions because it is timeless and not subject to immediate change.

Your appearances has to be balanced with the image of the company's other employees and that of the industry that you work in or are trying to enter. For example, if you are working toward becoming an artist or seeking to enter an art-related industry, then a more open and eclectic hair and dress style may fit perfectly into the norms and expectations of that culture. The key point is that veterans must allow their image and appearance to serve as a benefit and inducement to employment and not as a detractor.

Mistake 5: Not Asking for or Giving Help in the Career Transition

Military service and combat exposure create soldiers, sailors, marines, and airmen who are ready for battle. Members of the military possess independence, initiative, personal problem-solving abilities, endurance—and, at times, a decided lack of compassion for people who lack the ability to endure and suffer. These are great qualities for combat, but they need to be adjusted and controlled once back in the corporate business world. A focused mind, a determination to succeed no matter the cost, and a rigid exterior shell can be of great benefit in combat, but the business world requires greater openness, sharing, compassion, a desire to help, and a desire to be helped, in order to succeed.

Mistake 6: Not Fully Understanding the Potential Pitfalls of Corporate Culture

Corporate culture to a military person can be a daunting issue to understand and adapt to. The military, due to its long institutional history, extensive regulation, and high personnel turnover, largely operates in a consistent and uniform fashion between different units, geographies, and commander preferences. There will always be exceptions for military commands, but for the most part military units operate in a consistent, similar fashion. On the other hand, the culture of any corporation is entirely based upon its executive team, line of business, and history.

Corporate culture, as opposed to military culture, is largely unspoken and can often only be discerned through observation, quiet discussion, and experience. The veteran needs to approach a new organization, manager, and peer employees through a very open and unbiased perspective and not fall prey to the potential pitfalls of title, expected hierarchical relationships, or biased expectations of how a corporate culture should or must operate based upon a military culture or military hierarchy paradigm.

Observation and discussion with other veterans, especially those employed by the company for a longer period and those who served in the same service or combat zone, is the best method to understand the existing corporate culture. For example, how do people react when the boss walks in the room? Do people openly continue their conversations, or does everyone get quiet? How often do you see the boss or higher-level managers walking around and talking with employees? Can fellow employees accurately tell you what the business unit mission and goals are, or is there general misunderstanding of the strategy? Is the progress toward the business unit and company goals public, with open financial results, or are the strategic business results unpublished? How often are doors leading into offices open? Are doors and conversations often conducted behind closed doors? Do people leave the company or the business unit frequently for other opportunities? These types of verbal questions, combined with thoughtful observation, are a simple way to assess a corporate culture.

Ethics are another area of corporate culture that is potentially fraught with risk for the veteran employee. Most veterans take as an essential foundation of their day-to-day activities ethics such as honesty, the golden rule, general fairness, and an unbiased position regarding the backgrounds of other people. Business ethics and honesty can be more of a sliding scale of importance and priority within the corporate structure. Some organizations may stress honesty above all within the organization, but they may relax that standard and allow some less-than-honest practices when dealing with customers or other businesses. The point of vital importance is that veteran employees should not relax their own ethical standards, but they must fully understand the ethical standards and ethical practices of the organization for which they work. As a solid rule, if the veteran employee is uncomfortable with the ethics and ethical practices of the organization he works for, then he needs to find new employment and a corporate culture whose perspective and practices on the role of ethics in business are similar to his own. Sound ethical practices are the foundation of good business; but a veteran employee will struggle, most likely unsuccessfully, with attempting to transform corporate culture. The best option is to find a new opportunity and culture that matches your own personal preference for a corporate culture and ethical practices.

You need to leverage other veterans to gather their perspective and understanding of the company culture. A discussion on corporate culture with other veterans is especially helpful when trying to understand how your own personality and work style compare to those of immediate supervisors and their bosses. Supervisors' perspectives on ethics, communication styles, communication frequency, how much initiative employees can undertake, and how much risk employees can expose the company to are all excellent conversation topics to help you understand how your work personality compares to those of your supervisors. Again, observation and conversation are central to comparing and contrasting the work and personality style of superiors. The vast majority of superiors will never tell you directly, openly, and honestly the answers to these questions.

Your final area of understanding is office politics. Office politics were something of a problem in the military, but the use of centralized promotion boards, minimum time in specific ranks, pay caps, and a systematic promotion process takes away a great many, though not all, of the reasons for an office politics problem to arise. In the corporate environment, promotions, office space, pay raises, benefit packages, and key assignments can be decided in ways that may sometimes make the veteran employee, used to a centralized promotion system and uniform benefit packages, feel cheated and very uncomfortable. The best way to navigate office politics is not to participate in office politics, as tempting as it may be. Veteran employees need to focus on the execution of their business lines and let the results speak for themselves—along with their leadership, planning, and execution skills. In many regards, an organization that has a central focus on office politics probably has core ethical issues that will simultaneously push a veteran toward new opportunities. No one who plays serious office politics ever wins in the long term, and many corporations in which office politics were rampant—such as Enron, Aldelphia, and Govworks.com—ultimately failed.

Knowledge and understanding of the corporate culture is not something to complain about. Rather, knowing the corporate culture and how it operates is a way for you to successfully navigate through your projects, and navigate your career through the organization. The culture of an organization is not and never will be the military's culture, both for good and for bad. You must undertake a dedicated study of the company's corporate culture in terms of your own personal work culture compared to the company's culture of ethics, work practices, and office politics. An awareness of corporate culture, with its inherent benefits and drawbacks, will help you have a more successful career.

Mistake 7: Not Maintaining the "Can Do" Attitude

The "can do" positive attitude is one of the most compelling reasons why corporations choose to hire veterans. The "can do" attitude is marked by an adherence to innovation, contribution, learning, and personal initiative. Your "can do" attitude is a great replacement for corporate experience, and a strong, positive attitude further expands your own personal credibility in an organization. You should offer no apologies for your lack of corporate experience or lack of immediate industry knowledge and understanding of intricate corporate skills.

You need to maintain your "can do" positive attitude as you undertake your initial transition from the military to the corporate world. It is not uncommon for veterans to be depressed when their new corporate responsibilities are very different from their former military responsibilities. The retention of the "can do" attitude, a focus on learning, and a great work ethic will lead the veteran employee to success.

Summary

As a veteran, you are a great asset to any business. As either a current employee or a job candidate, you have to make a conscious effort to let your military experience and military training be a springboard to your current and future corporate career success. Success in your new career will come from leveraging your military experience and training to apply them to business, and from not allowing common veteran career transition mistakes disrupt or derail your career.

SECTION 2

PLAN

Plan

Thoughtful, detailed, timely, and decisive planning is as important to a successful business enterprise as it is to an important military operation. Business planners, like military planners, must provide enough information and detail for a plan to be successful, but not so much detail, analysis, and coordination that the strategic window for the business plan to be successful passes and the opportunity is missed. Good business planning must understand the competition and the marketplace environment, understand the company mission statement including supporting roles, use a structured process to anticipate and defeat the competition's moves, coordinate and synchronize the company's assets to fully achieve the business objectives, and use proven techniques to plan to mitigate risk to ensure a successful operation. Good planning therefore not only charts the company's actions, but also takes into account the market, the competition, the potential risks to the plan, and how to use all resources to ensure success.

CHAPTER 6

VETERAN LESSON 6: CREATE A CORPORATE PERIODIC INTELLIGENCE REPORT

Intelligence of the environment, the competition or the enemy, and any new or emerging developments is a central driver for both military and commercial operations. Although the intensity may vary slightly, the overall drive to have an accurate picture of what is happening today as well as foresight into the future, even if it may be slightly flawed, is incredibly valuable. U.S. Marines do not feel comfortable attacking and clearing a village when they do not have accurate intelligence on enemy troop numbers, fortification locations, enemy weapons available, and how the weather or moonlight will be the night of the operation. Likewise, corporate executives do not feel comfortable prior to the investment of $1 billion or more for a new factory employing hundreds of people when they do not know what the competition is doing, how customers feel, and if there are any emerging technologies that will make their new factory and product worthless. Timely, accurate, consistently researched, and consistently delivered intelligence is vital to the military and the corporate world so they can accurately understand, plan, implement, and adapt their plans to be successful.

Corporate business intelligence and military intelligence both have the same final goal: to create an accurate, timely, brief, complete, and directed picture of the environment and competition that allows a more successful implementation of the plan that brings about subsequent operational success. Veterans need to create, circulate, discuss, and improve these corporate business intelligence reports for their commercial organizations. With these intelligence reports, they are prepared to understand their business' competitive environment and lead their organization to success. As with all intelligence reports, understanding the operating environment and being able to translate that understanding into definitive action that yields successful business results is the ultimate goal of intelligence.

Introduction to the Corporate Periodic Intelligence Report

The Corporate Periodic Intelligence Report (CPIR) described in Figure 6 is a modification of military intelligence reports in the same respect that business intelligence enables corporate business professionals to achieve their business plans in the marketplace while simultaneously understanding what the competition is doing. There are four primary goals of a CPIR: (1) understand the market, (2) understand the competition's goals and means, (3) know customer value points, and (4) find new opportunities. The structure and detail of the CPIR is next. This format is an extensive version, but it can be modified as individuals/businesses see fit in order to conform closely to what they see as their primary business requirements.

Executive Summary for the Corporate Periodic Intelligence Report

The CPIR begins with an executive summary of all of the highlighted information for the major segments in the report. These should be intentionally brief items, and the executive summary should be a page at most in length. The purpose, as with all executive summaries, is for the report to draw out the most important information in each category for quick understanding and analysis.

1. **Executive Summary of Findings and Conclusion.** This section is intended to be a summary of the most important items in each of the five sections of the CPIR. These items should be directed toward the primary points of concern that the executive-level leadership would have for the strategy, direction, and execution of the company.
   a. **Top economic trends.** The top economic trends need to be targeted and adjusted so they reflect the most important items necessary for the successful operation of the business. In terms of a company that sells retail consumer products, macroeconomic variables such as changes in the rate of consumer lending, in the Consumer Price Index (CPI), or in the prices of important commodities (i.e., the price of grain per bushel for a cereal maker) would be essential to know to operate the company successfully.
   b. **Most damaging competitor actions to new and existing customers.** Tracking the most recent relevant activity of the competition is vital to ensure that the competition is being actively tracked for what they do, do not do, and how successful they are. In most corporate competitive situations, there will be restricted data, accurate and inaccurate customer statements, and selective coverage by the press. Finally, the scope of the analysis must include new customers as well as prospective customers for the company to stay fully ahead of the competition. For example, when Dell computer entered the server market in the 1990s, it was a significant departure from its personal computer products and services—only strategy that marked its competitive approach since its inception. This entry by Dell computer into

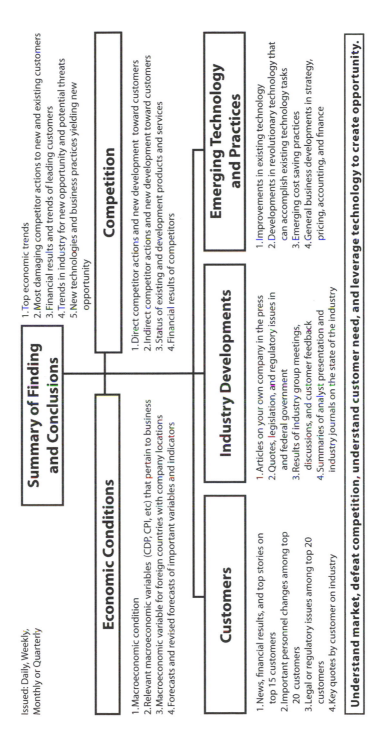

Issued: Daily, Weekly, Monthly or Quarterly

Summary of Finding and Conclusions

Economic Conditions

1. Macroeconomic condition
2. Relevant macroeconomic variables (CDP, CPI, etc) that pertain to business
3. Macroeconomic variable for foreign countries with company locations
4. Forecasts and revised forecasts of important variables and indicators

Industry Developments

1. Articles on your own company in the press
2. Quotes, legislation, and regulatory issues in and federal government
3. Results of industry group meetings, discussions, and customer feedback
4. Summaries of analyst presentation and industry journals on the state of the industry

Competition

1. Top economic trends
2. Most damaging competitor actions to new and existing customers
3. Financial results and trends of leading customers
4. Trends in industry for new opportunity and potential threats
5. New technologies and business practices yielding new opportunity

1. Direct competitor actions and new development toward customers
2. Indirect competitor actions and new development toward customers
3. Status of existing and development products and services
4. Financial results of competitors

Emerging Technology and Practices

1. Improvements in existing technology
2. Developments in revolutionary technology that can accomplish existing technology tasks
3. Emerging cost saving practices
4. General business developments in strategy, pricing, accounting, and finance

Customers

1. News, financial results, and top stories on top 15 customers
2. Important personnel changes among top 20 customers
3. Legal or regulatory issues among top 20 customers
4. Key quotes by customer on industry

Understand market, defeat competition, understand customer need, and leverage technology to create opportunity.

Figure 6.1. Design of the Corporate Periodic Intelligence Report.

computer servers was a significant competitive event for IBM, Sun, HP, and Compaq, all of which were already selling servers. Companies need to track these significant competitive events so they can be alerted to their first potential appearance, all the way through to understanding the details of their strategy and most likely execution strategy.

c. **Significant financial results and trends of leading customers.** Financial results are the base analysis of business, and all business people should devour as much of the financial condition of their competition as they can. Competitor's financial statements, such as the annual and quarterly earnings reports, are available from the company's website, usually in the investor's section; the Securities and Exchange Commission (SEC) website (www.sec.gov); and the business sections of most major media. Additionally, industry assessments from investment bankers, trade groups, industry organizations, and specific industry sector financial analysts present an array of good analysis for determining the success and likelihood of the competitive threat.

d. **Trends in industry for new opportunity and potential threats.** Following the major happenings and trends in an industry helps identify what could be the path to the future or highlights a customer frustration or new customer requirement that will drive change in the future. Apple computer with the iPod is an excellent example of a company leveraging a new trend in the industry. Apple saw the success that Sony and others had with the portable CD player and felt that it could improve on this model of providing music for consumers outside of music CDs. Industry trend monitoring helps ensure that a company's strategy is on the correct course.

e. **New technologies and business practices yielding new opportunity.** For example, when Google launched Google Docs, it was hardly a threat to Microsoft's dominance of office productivity software. However, Google's embrace of a Web-based version of corporate productivity software signaled the important rise of newer netbook-based laptop computers and their use on high-speed Internet connections for application software as opposed to software based on a computer's hard drive. New technology monitoring helps ensure that a company's strategy is on the correct course.

2. **Economic Conditions.** Macroeconomic conditions are best understood in terms of both statistics and personal anecdotes. In terms of statistics, the U.S. Department of Treasury, the U.S. Department of Labor, and private companies such as Global Insight all supply macro and micro economic variables that describe the condition of the economy. The problem for most businesses is to understand which economic variables are relevant to their success.

a. **Text-based descriptions of macroeconomic conditions.** This should be a general description and summary of the major economic trends that most directly influence the success of the business. This can include snippets from major policy speeches, leaders from foreign countries, or other internal national and regional economic leaders that are relevant to the operation of the business.

b. **Relevant macroeconomic variables (CDP, CPI, etc.) that pertain to business.** For example, a retailer may focus on macroeconomic trends such as consumer confidence, the Consumer Price Index (CPI) for relative prices, or average rates for consumer credit cards. All of these macroeconomic variables have a direct relation to the business operation, which makes them valuable.

c. **Macroeconomic variables for foreign countries with company locations.** These can be the same variables as 2b but applied to the country of business focus. Again, these macroeconomic variables should be directly relevant and associated to the operation of the business and/or how customers purchase the products and services.

d. **Forecasts and revised forecasts of important variables and indicators.** The U.S. Department of Labor, the U.S. Census Bureau, Global Insight, and the U.S. Treasury all provide macroeconomic forecasts.

3. **The Competition.** An understanding of where the competition is in terms of new products and services, new customer activity, new initiatives, financial performance, and strategic initiatives.

a. **Direct and indirect competitor actions and new developments that target customers.** These are new sales initiatives that directly target the company's customers as well as potential new customers. These could be announcements of sales, price increases or decreases, a new advertising campaign, or new customer announcements. Indirect actions are announcements of additional distributors that will carry the competitor's products or credit offered through financial institutions to help the competition's customers finance their product or service purchases.

b. **Status of existing and developing products and services.** These are new product introductions as well as modifications, additions, subtractions, and introductions to the competitor's line of products and services.

c. **Financial results of competitors.** These are the publicly announced earnings results available from the competition's website, the Securities and Exchange Commission (SEC) website as well as industry trade groups and local media articles.

4. **Customers.** During counterinsurgency warfare, it is vital to take and maintain the perspective of the population for all military actions and planned military actions. In counterinsurgency, once the population takes your side, the enemy can no longer use the population to hide. The acceptance of the local population and its support of the military force are vital to success. For a commercial business, as in counterinsurgency warfare, it is vital that the corporation truly embodies the perspective of its current and future customers to ensure all business activities are directed toward meeting and exceeding customer needs. The creation of an "intelligence report" to keep abreast of existing customer and planned customer events and influences is vital to ensure your company keeps meeting customer needs and stays ahead of the competition.

a. **News, financial results, and top stories on top 10 customers.** This is a list of all of the major news stories, financial results from company and SEC filings, and any other additional information on the customers.

b. **Important personnel changes among top 10 customers.** This is any publicly or privately announced changes in the management team with which the company interacts. This should also include senior executives in the customer's company since these may have a significant impact on company business activities.

   c. **Legal or regulatory issues among top 10 customers.** This is a list of any changes in laws or government regulations from the local, state, federal, or international level that positively or negatively affects how the customer does business.

   d. **Key quotes by the top 10 customers in industry publications.** These are telling quotes that reveal concern, business direction or strategy in the customer's business, feelings about other companies, or signs of a pending change in business operations.

5. **Industry Developments.** An understanding of new initiatives, research, government policy, legal issues, new competitive pressures, and customer trends that drive the direction of the industry.

   a. **Articles on your own company in the press.** This is a collection of major positive and negative news stories from the popular press and industry publications that describe the company's business operations, management, and direction.

   b. **Quotes, legislation, and regulatory issues in local to federal government.** This is any past, present, or future laws, regulations, or court decisions that affects the company's primary operations. These should be both positive and negative stories.

   c. **Results of industry group meetings, discussions, and customer feedback.** These could be minutes from industry meetings, press releases, and other insights that describe how the company stands in the industry and among major industry customer groups.

   d. **Summaries of analyst presentations and industry press on the state of the industry.** These news articles and analyst documents describe the overall future and direction of the industry. This is a location to describe possible new business lines as well as business lines that are dying off.

6. **Emerging Technology and Practices.** The focus on emerging technology as well as new business practices identifies technology that will radically change how business is conducted today and in the future. The examination of new technology is primarily driven by how does the invention, application, or implementation of new technology improve existing business opportunities, create new business opportunity, or make existing business practices obsolete.

   a. **Improvements in existing technology.** This would be new developments in an existing production process that makes the process faster, less expensive, or of higher quality. For example, the implementation of Global Positioning Systems (GPS) in trucks that deliver small packages to households and businesses, when paired with mapping and traffic pattern analysis software, improved efficiency, promoted better on-time performance, and was a greater value to customers from their package delivery provider. It was still the same business process, but new technology made the existing process better.

   b. **Developments in revolutionary technology that can accomplish existing technology tasks.** Developments in revolutionary technology would be ways that make existing processes obsolete while still accomplishing the underlying performance requirements for customers.

   c. **Emerging cost-saving practices.** The use of solar panels on factories to handle surge electricity production for manufacturing is an example of a technology being applied to help reduce costs.

d. **General business developments in strategy, pricing, accounting, and finance.** These are new processes or developments that improve the efficiency of business practices. This could be new academic or business trends for strategy designs, pricing methodologies, or other steps that help companies make more money, save money, or deliver greater value to customers.

Coverage Period for the Corporate Periodic Intelligence Report

These reports contain a significant level of detail that translates into a great deal of background work, research, fact checking, and source determination to make the CPIR a valuable and useful source of competitive intelligence. Depending on the availability of source data and the frequency with which that data are made available, the CPIR would be published on a weekly or monthly basis. The sheer breadth of this report would be a struggle to refresh on a daily basis. For intervals longer than a monthly basis, this report would be too old and the information dated to be relevant to a competitive or industry response.

Another option is to maintain a Web-based CPIR that has a regular publication schedule from weekly to monthly as well as back issues. This allows information to be post or updated as it is received, yet still maintains an archived portion that allows back research. Finally, ensure that you follow any restrictions for posting outside sources in any manner that may violate the terms of use of copyright law. The proper and respectful use of intellectual property is an absolute requirement for the CPIR.

A Note of Caution on the Gathering and Use of Competitive Intelligence

Military members, especially those with formal military education in intelligence and intelligence gathering, may be tempted to employ some of their former intelligence gathering skills to use as a source or sources for the CPIR. The use of intelligence techniques to gather competitive intelligence must, at all times, be able to pass the "news test."

The "news test" is, if your actions became public on your local TV news station, in the *Wall Street Journal*, or in the *New York Times*, would your actions reflect poorly on your company? For example, if you created a CPIR that placed information into categories from open sources, such as newspapers, magazines, and recent books, and you used that information in a consistent and truthful basis in the CPIR, then most news organizations would praise your resourcefulness and initiative. However, if your way to learn about your competition's cost-reduction program was to dumpster dive for documents outside their offices, bribe your suppliers for information, or tried to create friendships with the competition's employees, then your actions in the public eye would be viewed as anticompetitive, possibly illegal, and certainly damaging to the public and market perception of your company.

Summary

Good corporate intelligence identifies the primary questions in the markets your company serves, compiles the raw data from all the main sources of information, makes sense of all the sources, and then provides a regular and readable report to the broadest audience possible. This way, the corporate audience is well-informed on all of the major events and activities in the marketplace. The use of questionable methods and sources does far more damage to the company looking for the information than the value of the information procured. Good intelligence and good ethics can go hand-in-hand to provide your company with the best possible indicators of the competition as well as the marketplace's action.

CHAPTER 7

VETERAN LESSON 7: UNDERSTAND YOUR COMPANY'S MISSION STATEMENT

Mission statements are important because they provide a guideline, a vision, and a path to success for the organization that can be easily, quickly, and completely understood by all levels, from line worker to senior executive. A mission statement, whether corporate or military, is a succinct but complete statement of what the organization intends to accomplish, how it will accomplish this, and the overall sequence of the mission.

Mission statements in the military are a collection of "Who, what, when, where, and why" statements. The mission statement for military units, in its simplest form, drives the entire direction of a military unit toward its stated goal. An example of a military mission statement is as follows:

> The 75th Infantry Division [WHO] attacks to destroy enemy forces [WHAT] on Objective PANTHER [WHERE] no later than 0300 hours on January 17, 2008 [WHEN], in order to open up Highway 7 to provide humanitarian relief and support to the citizens located in City X [WHY].

When a military unit begins planning a mission, the mission statement is the first thing that every soldier in the unit must know in order to carry out their tasks in support of accomplishing the mission. Military organizations inherently understand that you must begin with the end in mind. The mission statement is a perfect example of a way to ensure that everyone in the unit understands what needs to be achieved in order to be successful. For a military commander, the knowledge that every soldier or marine understands the goal and purpose of what they are doing is essential to overcome the thousands of changes and adaptations that military units must perform in order to be successful. In order to accomplish the mission, military units may need to make hundreds of changes to their operational plans every day, due to the direct or indirect effects of weather, environment, political considerations, lack of resources, and enemy action. A simple, understandable, and complete mission statement ensures that the organization understands its objective and what they are working toward, even as they deal with changes to their basic plans and changes in their operating environment.

Military Use of Mission Statements

Military history provides an excellent framework for understanding the vital importance of the mission statement to successful mission execution and success. During the Korean War, a unit of the U.S. Army, Task Force Faith, was pursuing the retreating North Koreans along the eastern edge of the Chosin Reservoir, deep inside North Korea. The mood of the U.S. Army soldiers was ecstatic. The operation was going well, enemy resistance was light, and everyone hoped that the unit would be pulled back to Japan by Christmas. However, due to a variety of circumstances, Task Force Faith lost focus on their combat mission and reduced their focus on security. The results were catastrophic for Task Force Faith; it ran head-on into the attacking Chinese Communist forces when they invaded North Korea in late November 1950. The lesson is simple: To win, all soldiers and resources must understand and be focused on the same objective.

Corporate Use of Mission Statements

Corporate mission or purpose statements are equally telling examples of what the company is and strives to be. The following example, from Proctor and Gamble, provides an excellent example of the strategic direction and goals provided to the employees of the company:

The Procter and Gamble Mission Statement

We [WHO] will provide branded products and services of superior quality and value [WHAT] that improve the lives of the world's consumers [WHERE], now and for generations to come [WHEN]. As a result, consumers will reward us with leadership sales, profit and value creation, allowing our people, our shareholders and the communities in which we live and work to prosper [WHY].[1]

Commercial organizations demand the exact same use and understanding of a mission statement that the military does. Everyone in the organization, even at the lowest level, must understand his or her role and purpose, and how he or she fits into the larger company mission and its success. Just as in a military unit, the larger the company, the harder it is to constantly issue new orders and instructions to adapt tasks as the environment changes. A company with a good, well-understood, simple mission statement will be able to react effectively to changes in the competition, the marketplace, customer preferences, and the environment, because all employees understand the company's goals and can adapt their actions to ensure the success of the company's mission.

The Military-to-Commercial Mission Statement Process

Often, an employee will have to dissect or create a mission statement in order to fully understand how and why to best execute the company's mission and provide the highest level of quality products and services to that company's customers. The Military-to-Commercial Mission Statement Process is composed of six steps:

Step 1. Who—The commercial organization implementing the business plan.
Step 2. What—The business objective to be accomplished.
Step 3. When—The deadline or goal for the business plan to be accomplished.
Step 4. Where—The market geographies or primary target markets for the business plan.
Step 5. Why—The overall purpose to be achieved by a successful business plan.
Step 6. How—The necessary sub-steps that the business must accomplish to fulfill its mission statement.

For example, here is the mission statement analysis of a fictional express oil change company:

Fictional Mission Statement Example—Express Motor Oil Xchange

The mission of Express Motor Oil Xchange [WHO] will provide a premium automobile servicing experience for customers' basic automotive maintenance [WHAT] during peak and off-peak hours [WHEN] to working men and women, and busy families, throughout the United States and Canada [WHERE] in order to provide our customers with an automotive maintenance experience they will repeat due to service quality, speed, value, and convenience [WHY].

This mission statement for Express Motor Oil Xchange is typical of many small businesses in the United States—a small business in a highly competitive and high-demand industry attempting to differentiate itself to the customer through superior service and quality. You can make monumental improvements to small businesses when you combine the discipline, planning, preparation, and training of the military with the passion and drive of the business creator.

Step 6: How—Supporting Steps and Actions to Accomplish Mission Statement

Following the creation of a corporate mission statement, the employees and management of the company will need to conduct an analysis of the mission statement by breaking it apart in order to ensure that the company's operations reflect the complete line of services and value points. The danger is that if this analysis is not done, then the company risks disappointing all of its major stakeholders: shareholders, management, employees, customers, and the community. Only when a company's mission statement is in alignment with the actual value that it delivers to each segment of stakeholders can the company be successful.

Figure 7.1 is an example of the supporting steps and actions for Express Motor Oil Xchange to accomplish in order to be successful in its mission statement.

Company Mission Statement Analysis Example — Oil Xchange

Mission Statement Component	Who	What	When	Where	Why
Parts of Mission Statement	Working men, women, and busy families	Premium care servicing experience for their basic routine automotive maintenance	During our peak and off peak hours	Throughout the United States and Canada	An automotive maintenance experience they will repeat due to service quality, speed, value, and convenience
Supporting Steps and Actions to Accomplish Mission Statement	1. Target market analysis 2. Precise addresses to market to customers 3. Proximity of major businesses to Oil Xchange for advertising	1. Knowledge of car service for major automobiles 2. Parts on hand for repairs 3. Sufficient staffing for quick, quality repairs	1. Knowledge of area driving patterns 2. Extra staffing on weekend and lunch to cover "surges" in demand 3. Open on holidays to meet demand of target market	1. Growth locations by city and within cities 2. Knowledge of competition and their location, hours, etc 3. Proximity of major businesses to Oil Xchange for special deals	1. Use of customer survey to ensure customers satisfied. 2. Selective use of coupons to ensure value and mitigate competition risks. 3. Analysis of customer repeat business patterns to ensure loyalty.

Figure 7.1 Fictional Mission Statement Example of Express Motor Oil Xchange.

64

Company Mission Statement Analysis

Mission Statement Component	Who	What	When	Where	Why
Parts of Mission Statement					
Supporting Steps and Actions to Accomplish Mission Statement					

Figure 7.2 Company Mission Statement Analysis Worksheet.

The simple analysis of the fictional mission statement in Figure 7.1 provides great insight into what the business must do in order to be successful. The creation of an identifiable customer segment in terms of addresses, professions, annual incomes, etc., is vital in order for Express Motor Oil Xchange to identify where these customers live so they can create and implement a direct mail campaign. Furthermore, once the precise demographics of the target market customer base is identified, Express Motor Oil Xchange can more accurately determine the kinds and quantities of cars the customer base owns so they can be serviced quickly, accurately, and well. Finally, business assessment tools such as customer surveys, the use of coupons to encourage new customers, and financial analyses to ensure that customers are returning regularly, will ensure that the business is financially successful, reaching the correct market, and ensuring customers' repeat business.

In Figure 7.2, the company mission statement analysis worksheet can be employed for any business, from a global corporation to a small business.

Summary

Mission statements, whether military or corporate, demonstrate to customers, employees, shareholders, management, and the community on a daily basis what the company is here to do and why the company is doing it. It is vital in a company of any size, from a small business to a global corporation, that all of the supporting steps and actions that the company needs to take to successfully complete its mission be resourced, planned for, and undertaken. If there is a shortfall, then the company needs to add additional resources, or restate or redefine its mission statement to ensure that the company can fully address the requirements of the mission statement. The true test of a successful mission statement and the associated support steps and actions are the financial returns and market growth of the company.

In the military, success of a mission was sometimes clear and easy to define. If, at the end of the battle, I am standing on the objective, then I was clearly successful in my attack mission. For a corporate enterprise, if the company over time is delivering a product that meets the need of the target market customer base in a manner that is consistently superior to the competition, earns a profit that satisfies management and shareholders, satisfies the employee base with pay and benefits, and ensures that the community and environment are not harmed, then this company is fulfilling its mission statement to a very high degree.

Mission statements are enormously valuable compasses for corporations to navigate the churning, shifting waters of the marketplace. However, in order for the corporate mission statement to be of the most value, corporations must delve down into the precise primary and secondary tasks that the company must perform successfully in order to execute the mission statement successfully. Veterans and their knowledge of this essential military tool make them ideal to help guide the company in the mission statement process.

Note

1. Procter and Gamble Purpose, Values, and Principles statement, http://www.pg.com/company/who_we_are/ppv.shtml, accessed May 13, 2009.

CHAPTER 8

VETERAN LESSON 8: USE THE WAR GAME PROCESS

An extremely valuable tool the military uses to plan and modify its operations is the "war game" process. The war game process is a simple concept; essentially, it can be viewed as a large-scale game of Risk. In a war game, the military arrays all of its primary and supporting forces against the enemy and then enacts the phases of its operation while doing its best to "play" the enemy and anticipate the enemy's effects on the friendly plan. The outcome of the war game process is a military operation that has been tested against the expected enemy's actions to create a better plan that will succeed. This ability to model the competition to your business is exceptionally valuable to the successful execution of a business strategy.

The goal of the war game process is to use the dry run execution of your draft business plan to determine your competitor's strengths and weaknesses, and then take that information to create an improved business plan that has the highest chances of success. The war game process is intended to be a very detailed interplay of your business plan versus the competition to ensure that the friendly business plan has the best chance of success.

Organization of the War Game Process

The war game process can be accomplished with almost any level of resources. At the end of a war game, the military will have fully exercised its operational plan, fully described the expected enemy actions and counteractions to its plan, and inserted additional steps into its plan to counteract new or unexpected steps that were revealed about the enemy during the war game. A war game is a large-scale "dry run" of a draft plan so problems with a plan can be anticipated early on and solutions implemented ahead of time to ensure the success of the plan. For the vast majority of businesses, there is virtually no existing process for a business unit to systematically "fight" a business plan and record the expected results, and then implement changes to a business plan to ensure success.

The execution of a military war game follows a systematic process that breaks down the plan and resources involved into component parts over time, then plays these assets against the competition, and records the expected outcomes. The military leader and staff place their forces and supporting elements on a table or computer screen and then start moving the pieces in accordance with their draft plan. A separate group of officers, led by the intelligence officer, plays the enemy, and acts and reacts to try to defeat the friendly force as best they can. A third element serves as a recorder and judge to record, evaluate, and decide the results of engagements as well as record what modifications to make to the plan as the war game plays out. The result of the war game process is an updated plan that reduces the effectiveness of enemy action and gives the friendly military element the best possible chance of success.

In the commercial world, the war game process has excellent potential to determine likely competitor consequences to new product introductions, store openings, price changes, and interactions with customers. For example, let's say you own a small fast-food restaurant located in close proximity to the opening of a new store for a direct competitor. Using the war game process, you can consider business factors such as store hours, traffic patterns, menu items, and prices for similar food items and determine what the most likely effects from the new store will be. Additionally, you can look at what your competition's most likely strategy will be in opening its new store and how you need to respond.

Commercial War Game Process Steps

The war game process is divided into four distinct phases to help the organization thoroughly understand the effects of both friendly and competitor activity while ensuring consensus on required changes to the plan and anticipation of the competitor's most likely actions. The war game process consists of four phases:

> Step 1: Prepare for the War Game
> Step 2: Execute the Initial Phase of the Friendly Business Plan and Determine the Most Likely Competitor Reaction
> Step 3: Friendly Counteraction to Offset the Effectiveness of the Competitor Reaction
> Step 4: Supplement the Draft Business Plan with the Successful Friendly Action and Counteractions from the War Game

The application of these phases ensures that the war game process is disciplined, timely, organized, and consistent to deliver the most likely competitor actions, refine the company's business plan, and determine the best steps for a successful business plan execution. Figure 8.1 outlines the commercial war game steps.

Commercial War Game Planning Worksheet

Date _____

Commercial Strategy & Key Execution Steps:

Competitor #1 Commercial Strategy & Key Execution Steps:

Competitor #2 Commercial Strategy & Key Execution Steps:

Competitor #3 Commercial Strategy & Key Execution Steps:

Commercial Plan Wargame

	Time +1	Time +2	Time +3	Time +4	Time +5	Time +6	Time +7	Time +8	Time +9	Time +10	Time +11	Time +12
Company Base Strategy												
Company Asset #1 Action												
Company Asset #2 Action												
Company Asset #3 Action												
Competitor #1 Reaction												
Competitor #2 Reaction												
Competitor #3 Reaction												
Company Asset #1 Counter Action												
Company Asset #2 Counter Action												
Company Asset #3 Counter Action												

Commercial Plan Wargame Results

	Time +1	Time +2	Time +3	Time +4	Time +5	Time +6	Time +7	Time +8	Time +9	Time +10	Time +11	Time +12
Units Sold												
Revenue												
Cost												
Net Income												
Avg Revenue Unit												
Avg Cost Unit												

	Time +1	Time +2	Time +3	Time +4	Time +5	Time +6	Time +7	Time +8	Time +9	Time +10	Time +11	Time +12
Draft Changes to Company Plan												

Figure 8.1 Commercial War Game Planning Worksheet.

Step 1: Prepare for the War Game

Preparation for the war game process consists of five major steps. The steps are as follows:

Step 1. Selecting the appropriate corporate players for the business plan war game.

Step 2. Deciding on a war game format to record and evaluate the war game results.

Step 3. Determining the evaluation or assessment criteria to determine if the friendly business plan succeeds or fails.

Step 4. Selecting an independent judge(s) to evaluate the effectiveness of the friendly and competitor actions.

Step 5. Arraying the friendly and competitor resources that will carry out the plan.

These five steps create an execution and evaluation framework for the war game that allows decisions to be made, disagreements to be evaluated, and the war game process to progress in an effective manner. A great danger in the war game process is that if an effective evaluation and judging framework is not decided upon, the war game process might collapse under its own weight as disagreement breaks out over the effectiveness of the plan, what the plan is, and how to evaluate the plan's effectiveness. The thorough preparation of a war game creates an atmosphere of learning and pointed intellectual discussion that will allow the plan with the best chance of success to emerge.

The first step of the war game is to have as many representatives from different commercial and operational areas of the business as possible. Marketing, sales, finance, operating, supply, business development, and strategic planning are just some of the people to have in place for the war game process. Critical suppliers, consultants, and other trusted business partners may want to be present for the entirety or for portions of the process. There should be an appropriate level of representation from local, regional, and national interests based on the level of the business plan. If the purpose of the war game is to determine how the competition and consumers will react to a national price change, then the representation should be from the national and regional levels. The representation of the appropriate people for the war game must mirror those that will carry out the business plan. If there is a disconnect between war gaming and business plan execution, then the war game results will be flawed or useless.

The second step of the war game process is to select or decide on a format to record the results of the process. The use of a systematic, consistent, and disciplined process is important to keep the war game going as well as to ensure that all of the important lessons and findings from the war game are included in the final business plan. The Commercial War Game Planning Worksheet offers a ready-made solution for the commercial war game process. First, the broad outlines of the friendly and competitor plans and strategies must be written out and decided upon so the war game plan can proceed. This seemingly simple step of clearly defining the plan, purpose, and execution steps of the friendly and competitor business plans is enormously valuable. The value lies in ensuring everyone understands the draft plan of execution for the friendly business plan as well as ensuring that the competitor's strategy is known and understood.

The third step in preparing for the war game is to determine the evaluation or assessment criteria to help identify if the friendly business plan succeeds or fails. This step is essentially selecting an indicator or indicators to determine if the business plan is succeeding or failing. For the majority of business plans, indicators such as revenue, number of customers served, customer satisfaction rankings, customer survey results, market share versus the competition, the overall profit margin, and amount of net income or profit earned would be seen as typical indicators of success for a business plan. A key to creating the success indicators is to ensure that there is a clear definition of what the success metric is, how often the data is gathered, and that the use of this metric passes the common sense test. For example, if a customer survey is used to gauge success, then questions such as how often does the survey go to customers, how do customers receive the survey, does the survey go only to customers that have had a problem, and so on should be considered. Indicators are a great asset to determine success, but great care must go into the collection, storage, and use of the data to ensure that the indicator accurately and truly reflects the status of the business.

The third step in war game preparation also includes a decision on the recording format to use in the process. The recording of events, competitor reaction, and friendly company counteraction is a vitally important step to ensure the successful use of the war game process to improve the primary business plan. The use of a systematic recording tool or worksheet ensures the war game process remains on track as well as captures all of the lessons learned for the primary business plan. There should be a dedicated recorder as well as note taker to record the results of war game encounters as well as notes on adjustments to the primary plan. Finally, the recorder also can track any additional assets that are required for the business plan's execution as well as identify any redundant assets that are no longer required.

The fourth step in war game preparation is to select an independent judge or judges to evaluate the effectiveness of the friendly and competitor actions. This is a vital step because war games can easily break down when there is no clear-cut decision on who "won" an engagement between friendly and enemy forces. Having an impartial judge or judges evaluate the plan's effect on both friendly and competitor businesses is key to a good war game. An independent, impartial, and fair judge makes the war game process run smoothly and ensures the best use of everyone's time in improving the draft plan for a successful execution.

The fifth and final step in the war game preparation phase is to array all friendly and competitor resources that will carry out the plan. This is an important step because it reminds all parties to create a complete inventory and list all available business resources they can use in the war game process and the execution of the business plan. Arraying all available assets is vital because it provides an instant "double check" that the business plan incorporates all the assets. Once the preparation and organization for the war game has been completed, the process can begin.

Step 2: Execute the Initial Phase of the Friendly Business Plan and Determine the Most Likely Competitor Reaction

The war game process at its core is a study of how well the friendly plan will succeed and how the competition will react to the friendly business plan. The war game process works best when the friendly business plan has been divided into distinct phases that can be "played" in a series of moves against the competition. Examples of business phases are: (1) preparation for new store opening, (2) the initial one to four weeks of a new store opening, (3) the first year of a new store opening, and (4) special business events such as Christmas holiday sales and other special sales or high-traffic events. Other events that can be segmented for a war game process are unique and high-impact business events such as the company's reaction to a price increase or decrease, and the expected competitor reaction when a business seizes a key customer from the competition.

Once the business plan has been divided into usually no more than four distinct phases, the war game members will form teams to represent the friendly plan and the competition. There also will be a person or people who will serve as a judge to evaluate the outcome and effects of the friendly plan and the competitor's reaction. To keep the war game process productive and moving along, the judge and war game teams should establish timelines for their initial friendly action, competitor reaction, judge evaluation, and points learned. These four blocks can be divided into 15-minute segments so a four-phase business plan could be initially war gamed in less than four hours.

As the war game process begins, each team needs to use precise actions and dates to provide clarity to the plan's execution and to formulate a precise competitive response. For example, in the opening of a new retail establishment, the friendly company would state for its action, "On November 15, 2009, we plan to open Chris's Used CDs at 11 AM. Our hours of operation will be from Monday through Saturday from 11 AM to 10 PM. We will price our used CDs as follows . . ." This specific action- and date-driven format fully exercises the business plan and lets the war game team playing the competition understand fully to formulate their reaction.

The war game teams for both the friendly company and the competitors should be as multifunctional as possible to exercise all aspects of the friendly business plan as well as the full extent of the competition's reaction. A good multifunctional team includes representatives from operations, finance, marketing, sales, transportation, and purchasing or supply functions. Depending on the project, information technology, legal, research and development, investor relations, and corporate communications may also be part of the teams if they will play a major role in the business plan. The essential aspect of war game team formulation is to have as many representatives as possible from the major corporate functions who will execute the business plan. However, the war game team should also be kept as small as possible to enable the process to be nimble and constructive so all competitive aspects of the results are mentioned.

Step 3: Friendly Counteraction to Offset the Effectiveness of the Competitor Reaction

Once the company war gamers have run through the process of the friendly action and the competitor's initial reaction, the company has to determine what the friendly counteraction will be to offset the effectiveness of the competition's reaction. In the vast majority of cases, the friendly counteraction needs to be an action that will, in the best case, forcefully mitigate the competitor's initial reaction. For example, let's use the example of a business plan scenario in which a computer company is planning to build a new computer assembly factory. The location for the new factory will be located geographically in the middle of a base of computer component suppliers. The competitor's reaction to this factory was to establish a computer assembly factory in this same area. The counteraction to the competition's planned factory is to seek a long-term and high total percentage of the computer parts suppliers' output. This way, if the competitor does establish this factory, then the company has denied them access to the computer supplier manufacturing base. This friendly counteraction of long-term supplier contracts ultimately defeats the competitor's purpose for locating their computer assembly factory in the middle of the supplier base, the original rationale for their strategy.

The friendly counteraction must seek to maintain the company in a better competitive and commercial position toward customers, suppliers, and the financial goals of the primary business plan. Activities that destroy commercial value that is unnecessary, such as discounts or aggressive, punitive actions toward suppliers that have temporarily sided with the competition, will not keep the company in a better commercial or competitive position. The friendly counteraction needs to directly target the reasons why the competitor's reaction was effective to begin with.

As with the initial war game steps, the friendly counteraction must be precise in its specific actions, what is involved, who will do it, and the date that the action will begin and end. This specific description of actions is vital to the use of friendly counteractions as a component of the primary business plan. Good counteractions can often be prebuilt into the initial business plan so that the competition finds itself facing an insurmountable plan from the beginning. At this point, once a phase of the business plan has been successfully war gamed and all the relevant lessons captured, discussed, and recorded, the war game teams go back to the start of the War Game Phase 2 and begin the process of friendly action, competitor reaction, and friendly counteraction through the remaining phases of the business plan.

Step 4: Supplement the Draft Business Plan with the Successful Friendly Action and Counteractions from the War Game

The final step in the war game process is to review and update the primary business plan with the knowledge learned and discussion points from the war game process. This final step is the most important because without the incorporation of the learning points from the war game into the draft business plan, the entire war game process has no purpose. The use of a recorder and an organized war game worksheet makes capturing all the lessons from the war game when they occur much easier. Additionally, the capture and incorporation of war game lessons into the business plan helps create a great deal of "buy–in" and acceptance of the war game, because all team members have had an opportunity to voice their opinion as well as incorporate their best opinion of what the competition will do.

Formal and Informal Commercial War Game Process

The four phases of the war game process previously described are used in the formal war game process. The formal process is used for large plans, when there is sufficient time, workers, and resources available for a dedicated, accurate, and intense dissection of a business plan against the competition. An informal war game process also can be used that incorporates all of the same four phases of the war game process. This informal war game process is intended to be used when fewer people, resources, and time is available, but the employees in charge of the business plan want the benefit of a war game process to reinforce their plan's success.

An informal war game process could be a group of people around a table running through the phases of their plan, anticipating the competition's reaction, and then creating additional steps in their business plan to reduce the effectiveness of the competition's expected actions. This is a war game process. Finally, the entire purpose of a war game process is to make an existing plan better by playing the plan against a realistic and determined competitor. If your war game process results in a better plan and improved execution as judged by your success indicators, then you have succeeded.

Common Mistakes in Commercial War Gaming

There are a number of very common mistakes in war gaming that can be easily avoided and prevented in order to have a productive and effective war game of the draft business plan. Listed are three of the top war game problems.

1. **Confusion on the Base Business Plan.** Often war game teams are unsure what the precise steps are in the draft business plan, so they are unsure how to completely enact the business plan. This lack of understanding of the draft plan leads to confusion. If people do not understand the plan, temporarily halt the war game and review the draft plan again.
2. **Disagreement on Effects of War Game Actions.** There can be exceptionally heated debates between the friendly and competitor war game teams on the effects of the actions by either of the groups. The use of independent judges and evaluators can quickly suppress these disagreements and keep the war game going. Use two or three independent judges to ensure a productive war game.
3. **Losing Focus on the War Game Results.** Often if war games are not well organized, the plan is not understood, or there are no war game judges present, war games break down and lose their focus. The use of a war game worksheet to record results, a strict timeline, a dedicated team, and frequent breaks keeps the war game effective and leads to good discussions that strengthen the draft plan.

Summary

The war game process is an excellent, cost effective, and quick way to test business plans for their effectiveness prior to execution. War games have a large number of structural rules that, when followed, keep the process timely, effective, and moving along. Good war games make draft business plans better because they fully incorporate the business' best opinions on what the competition will do to defeat their business plan and incorporate that knowledge to create safeguards and countermeasures to ensure the success of the business plan.

CHAPTER 9

VETERAN LESSON 9: USE THE MILITARY SYNCHRONIZATION MATRIX

The purpose of the military synchronization matrix is to align critical resources for a successful military operation at the decisive time and location in order to fully coordinate all resources that contribute toward a successful mission. For example, in attempting to breach an enemy defensive line, attack helicopters, artillery, smoke, medical support, reinforcements, communications equipment, and ammunition re-supply would be positioned to ensure maximum effectiveness at the precise time they were required in support of the attack. In all of the time leading up to the attack, each supporting arm would have its specific tasks and timings precisely defined so each would be ready to support the mission. When the attack commences, each combat element and supporting force will move together to bring maximum effects upon the enemy and ensure a successful mission. The synchronization matrix ensures that all military resources are prepared, positioned, and coordinated to support a successful mission outcome.

Corporations Synchronize Their Assets to Support Successful Commercial Operations

Businesses have the same requirements to coordinate and position all of their key resources to ensure the success of their business strategy. Ensuring that all of the company's financial, sales, marketing, and operating assets and personnel are coordinated is vital to the success of the business strategy. Major business events such as new product introductions, new store openings, product recalls, or reaction to a company crisis are all corporate business events that are vitally important in order for the company to perform successfully. However, for the company to perform these events successfully, it needs to coordinate a wide variety of business functions, personnel, and resources that may be located in different geographies, and ensure that they work together successfully. The military synchronization matrix can be used to assist in corporate asset coordination—which makes it much more likely for a business operation to succeed.

Purpose and Organization of the Commercial Synchronization Matrix

The commercial synchronization matrix is used to coordinate the events of a large number of different organizations or business functions that have to synchronize their actions and resources over a pre-established length of time in order to accomplish an important business goal. The preparations for and opening of a new retail store over a six-month period is a perfect example: functions such as merchandise supply, marketing, advertising, public relations, management, human resources, and finance all have to coordinate their actions down to the hour and minute that the store opens for the first time. If any business function or resource fails to coordinate and act in conjunction with any of the other business functions, then the entire project may not be a success and will almost certainly be disjointed, causing increased costs, decreased revenue, and a loss of customer satisfaction. Coordination and synchronization of all functions, employees, and resources is as vital to success in business as it is in the military.

Framework and Directions on the Commercial Synchronization Matrix

The business synchronization matrix follows a simple grid format (see Figure 9.1). Across the horizontal or X-axis, there is a timeline that starts from the position of the current date and leads to one or two weeks past the start or goal time of the business event. On the vertical or Y-axis, there is a listing of all the resources and business functions that are available to the team executing the business plan. The intersection of the X-axis of time and the Y-axis of the business function or resource forms a square in which the actions that the business function has to complete in the specified period are recorded. At the top of the X-axis, there should be a minor supporting event in the business plan that all parties can use to track the progress of the business plan and ensure that the supporting activities of the business functions remain focused on progression toward the business plan goals. The use of this format creates a simple, clear, and easily understood tool, so that every actor involved in supporting the business plan can see what has been done, what will be done, and to whom any specific action is assigned.

The Commercial Synchronization Matrix Process Steps

The business synchronization matrix should be introduced at a joint meeting between all of the business functions and the management team in charge of executing the business plan. At the meeting, the management team should review the overall business purpose and the rationale for the strategic business plan before

Synchronization Matrix Worksheet

Business Task: _____

As of: _____

	Time Period +1	Time Period +2	Time Period +3	Time Period +4	Time Period +5	Time Period +6	Time Period +7	Time Period +8	Time Period +9	Time Period +10	Time Period +11
Project Time Period Goal											
Business Group 1											
Business Group 2											
Business Group 3											
Business Group 4											
Business Group 5											
Business Group 6											
Business Group 7											
Business Group 8											

Figure 9.1 Commercial Synchronization Matrix Worksheet.

beginning a review of the business synchronization matrix and the responsibilities involved. Once the entire group understands the business plan and strategic business purpose, the management team can begin a general description of the entire business plan and major supporting activities over the entire planning, preparation, and execution times of the business plan. The creation of the commercial synchronization matrix has the following steps:

Step 1. Identify resources available to support the business plan.
Step 2. Identify major weekly events in the business plan.
Step 3. Meet with all resources to coordinate use in the business plan.
Step 4. Follow up to ensure implementation success.

Step 1: Identify Resources Available to Support the Business Plan

The first step is to conduct a brainstorming session with the business team to identify all the available and possible resources that can be used to support the business plan implementation. The business team may have dedicated assets assigned, such as specific marketing and operations personnel, to carry out the business plan. The business team will also have functions such as human resources, advertising, sales, and finance that they will have to share with other business teams. There will also be resources that the company does not own, but the planning team will nonetheless have to brainstorm for how to employ them. In the example of a planned retail store opening, the business team may be able to coordinate with public relations to have local public officials attend to raise the visibility of the event and attract even larger crowds of customers to the store. The business team needs to identify as many resources as possible that can be used to make the business implementation plan successful.

Step 2: Identify Major Weekly Events in the Business Plan

The next step is to identify the major weekly or daily events in the business plan. These weekly or daily events will then become the focus points for all the business activities to support the business plan. The business plan should be divided into areas of focus for each week that will then drive the synchronization and coordination efforts for all company resources each week. For example, in a retail store opening, four weeks prior to opening, the focus of the store for that week might be "soft opening preparation." The soft opening preparation tasks would have human resources confirming the hiring of new employees and establishing work schedules. Merchandise would have the store inventory deliveries scheduled and the store location for each item assigned. Advertising would have all of the advertising campaign coordinated for the grand opening, as well as initiating a "teaser" campaign to remind customers of the impending grand opening. The weekly major activities or focus events help each of the company's business support assets to fully and completely coordinate their weekly activities to ensure that the weekly focus event is successful. If each of the weekly business focus events is successful, the overall business plan implementation will be successful.

Step 3: Meet with All Business Assets to Coordinate Use in the Business Plan

The goal for this portion of the creation of the business synchronization matrix is to ensure that each supporting business function fully understands what they can and cannot perform, identify any questions or clarifications that are required, and reveal any other supporting activities that they need another business function to perform. Using the retail store opening example again, most stores perform a "soft" or quiet opening one to three weeks prior to their grand opening. During these "soft" openings, the management team fully tests the capabilities of the store to meet all of their required operational functions to the standard of the corporation. During these meetings, the business function of training may identify that they need to begin training eight weeks out from the grand opening and not four. This would lead to additional requirements from human resources for earlier hiring; the business would have to have employee uniforms ready in ten weeks, and so on. This period ensures that all business functions fully understand their role and provides time for them to identify any additional tasks or resources they need to complete the plan.

Step 4: Follow Up to Ensure Implementation Success

The follow-up meeting is the coordination phase and final design of the business synchronization matrix. In this meeting, which can last an entire day or several days depending on the scope and complexity of the business plan to be executed, the entire business synchronization matrix plan is confirmed. A best practice for these meetings is to set the room up in a U-shaped arrangement of tables, with a large screen and projector at the open portion of the U. This design enables all those present to see the others and gives them sufficient workspace for notes and other planning materials. The projection screen at the opening of the U should have a large blow-up of the synchronization matrix, and someone at the meeting should be designated ahead of time to show, modify, and confirm the business synchronization matrix as the plan changes.

Following this format, the group can open discussion of the supporting activities and timings and then ensure, using the projector, that the correct actions and timelines are captured. At the conclusion of the de-confliction meeting, the business team will have a copy of the business synchronization matrix that the entire group has seen and understands. The subsequent agreement on the business synchronization matrix may not be fully endorsed by all parties, but all parties will have had the opportunity and an open forum to voice their opinions and ensure their concerns were addressed.

Potential Shortcomings of the Business Synchronization Matrix

The first potential shortcoming in the business synchronization matrix process is failure to reach consensus. The business synchronization matrix requires, at a minimum, three separate meetings to be a success. The three meetings are (1) the initial overview meeting, (2) a detailed business function support planning meeting, and (3) a final coordination meeting in which the business synchronization matrix is confirmed. If there is insufficient planning time available, then the business synchronization matrix can be a less-than-valuable business execution tool, because it will not have the consensus of the business team leaders behind it—and there may also be a critical lack of timing, coordination, and synchronization in the business plan. Consensus and understanding among all parties involved in the execution of the business plan are essential in order to make the business synchronization matrix a worthwhile and efficient planning tool.

The second potential shortcoming in the business synchronization matrix process is a failure to have clearly defined and understood supporting activities. If the business team is new or has not worked together before, then there needs to be agreement so that every person understands the precise definition and scope of the supporting business activity. For example, on the final day, the supporting business activity may state "Open the store." A new or unfamiliar employee may read that as "Unlock the doors." Another, more seasoned, employee may read that as "Unlock the doors, have a final store cleaning the night before, confirm the day's employees two days prior, pick up cash for the registers in the morning," etc. For a business synchronization matrix to be very successful, there must be clear understanding and precision about what each business unit does.

The third and final potential shortcoming in the business synchronization matrix process is a corporate culture that does not value open communication. The business synchronization matrix requires open, honest, and clear corporate communication. None of the meetings, business planning tools, or business function involvement will make a plan successful if the leaders do not believe in the plan and inspire their supporting teams to make it a success. Furthermore, all plans, both military and business, are a starting point and quickly evolve as the market environment, competition, and resource availability change and fluctuate. The business synchronization matrix is the starting point of the plan, but all business team members must communicate what they have done, what they plan to do, and any problems involved, so that the plan remains on track and is a success. A business team that blindly follows a synchronization matrix may have a plan succeed, more through blind luck or an uncharacteristic lack of change in the business conditions, than through great planning, communication, and teamwork. Good business planning and clear, frequent, and simple communication is what creates great business execution.

Summary of the Value of the Commercial Synchronization Matrix

The business synchronization matrix is a tool to align available business functions and resources over a planned preparation and execution period to achieve a business plan. It is a simple and clear tool to precisely focus the resources of the corporation in a collaborative effort to meet the business objectives. Overall, for the business synchronization matrix to be a success, it requires clear and open communication in the planning and execution phases so that all parties' activities and timings are precisely defined, any shortcomings or problems are identified early, and the team openly communicates during the execution phase so they can quickly adapt to changes in the business environment, competition, or resource allocation.

CHAPTER 10

VETERAN LESSON 10: EMPLOY RISK MITIGATION

What is business risk? Business risk is any action or event from natural or manmade forces that threatens the continued successful operation of a business. For a military operation, success is achieving your mission objective in the specified time with as few casualties as possible and as much of your equipment intact as possible. Business success is as follows: the company is profitable; it possesses dedicated, loyal, and engaging employees; it retains employees through a fair wage and benefit; it has a growing base of customers with high customer satisfaction; it operates in a safe and environmentally friendly manner; and it has a diversified product and service portfolio that is ahead of the competition and is continuously being improved.

Employees at All Levels Must Plan to Mitigate Significant Business Risk

Risk is all things that threaten the success of a business enterprise. Risk can be a wet floor that causes employees to trip and injure themselves, as well as a complex commodity trading strategy that exposes the firm to crippling losses when the price of the traded commodity falls. The struggle for a corporation is how to determine its strategy to mitigate risk. After all, there are levels of risk that can simply not be mitigated. How can a courier company that delivers packages fully mitigate all the risk that comes from a rainstorm that slows traffic and prevents its drivers from all of their scheduled pickups and deliveries? Even if not all risk can be mitigated, there are a large number of activities that companies can do to reduce the risk to their operations and ensure they remain successful. A risk mitigation strategy helps a company prevent the risks it can and helps mitigate the effects of the risks that cannot be prevented.

A core function of what the management of a company is hired and retained to do is understand and mitigate risk. This applies equally, if not more, to military

Table 10.1 An Example of Business Risk and Risk Mitigation for Dell Computer

Initial Risk to Dell Computers	Commercial Risk Mitigation Technique
Oversupply and outdated component inventory (COST)	Use of just-in-time component purchasing and expedited transportation
No storefronts for consumer purchase of computers (REVENUE)	Use of mail, phone, and Internet consumer factory-to-home direct purchase model
Initial limited working credit line to finance computer component purchase (REVENUE)	Customers purchased computers prior to shipping, giving Dell a temporary "float" of cash to finance computer components

commanders and their staff. Risk management in the military was once viewed with skepticism. After all, what is a more inherently risk-filled profession than being a member of the military? However, military professionals have always recognized that creating operations that are less risk-filled is a core element of successful military operations. Indeed, risk mitigation for the military is a daily, if not hourly, or continuously occurring task. Weapons have safety devices, military forces conduct extensive reconnaissance to learn about the enemy-force capabilities and dispositions prior to an operation, medical care is extensively practiced, and all military forces train, train, and train to accomplish their assigned missions quickly, effectively, and under all weather and enemy conditions. Although military forces accept the fact that they cannot control the enemy, they absolutely reject the lack of control of all risk. Risk mitigation by military units is recognized as the hallmark of professional military forces. A military commander and a CEO both recognize that the loss of a soldier or the loss of a key customer, respectively (and not even close on the scale of importance), are regrettably understandable—if the loss comes from the enemy or from the competition—but utterly unforgivable if that loss could have been prevented by actions the military unit or company could have undertaken.

Risk and the measured taking of risks have long been key ingredients of successful businesses and military operations.

When Michael Dell began assembling personal computers in his room for friends and family at the University of Texas–Austin, he knew a little bit about risk and taking chances. Michael Dell took the risks of manufacturing computers and used all of these risks to create risk mitigation techniques to create a new business model (see Table 10.1). The Dell risk mitigation strategy helped create a new business model for Dell Computers.

Applying Military Risk Mitigation to Business

The company struggle is how to create a risk strategy that allows it to be the most successful, profitable company, but without having operations, products, or services that are so inherently risky that they undermine the complete success and health of the company. You can use the risk management process to insert risk mitigation practices into your daily operations that will help keep the company safe, profitable, and retaining highly satisfied customers through high quality goods and services. You can support their company's risk prevention and risk mitigation strategy by employing daily strategies to make company operations safer, less costly, and more satisfying to customers.

You can prevent risks to your company by following the military-to-commercial risk mitigation process:

1. Identify the business objective.
2. Identify the primary risks to the business objective.
3. Identify the likelihood and the severity of the risk.
4. Create a plan to implement the risk mitigation steps.

This four-step risk mitigation process, modeled loosely after the military's risk assessment process, allows you to create a cohesive risk mitigation action plan for your area of the business.

Overview of the Military-to-Commercial Risk Mitigation Process

The commercial risk mitigation worksheet is the framework for you to help mitigate risks in your area of the business (see Figure 10.1). The four steps of the commercial risk mitigation worksheet focus on identifying those areas most critical to the success of the business and on determining the best action plans and steps to reduce the potential effects on the business objective. For example, the business objective of "cost reduction" is used to identify threats that cause the base costs needed to manufacture, assemble, transport, administer, and market products and services for the company to become higher. There is always some type of annual cost inflation, but when the costs for products and services escalate faster than the revenue associated with the products and services, the eventual demise of the company is unavoidable. The end goal of the commercial risk mitigation worksheet is to identify the vulnerabilities to the company, define the solutions to ensure a successful business objective, and then create an actionable and effective plan for the risk mitigation item.

Step 1: Identify the Business Objective Exposed to Risk

The first step in the commercial risk mitigation process is to identify the business objective that could be exposed to risk. The business objectives are grouped into five key areas that support the overall effectiveness of the business. The five core business objectives are (1) cost reduction, (2) revenue maximization, (3) reduced effectiveness of competition, (4) safety improvements for employees and the public, and (5) employee effectiveness. Depending on the business or the commercial objectives, these areas could be expanded or reduced, but these five provide an excellent global view of business objectives that need to have risk mitigated for a successful business outcome. For example, a quality risk mitigation process could be added for a manufacturing or service company to address how to maintain and improve high quality in its products or services. A quality program is a reduction in the number

Commercial Risk Mitigation Worksheet

Business Task: _____   Date: _____

Step 1	Step 2	Step 3		Step 4	Review
Business Objective	**Primary Risks to the Business Objective**	**Likelihood of Risk Occurrence (low, medium, high)**	**Severity of Risk Occurrence (low, medium, high)**	**Plan to Implement Risk Mitigation Controls**	**Success Criteria to Evaluate Effectiveness of Risk Mitigation Plan**
Cost Reduction				WHO: WHAT: WHEN: WHERE: WHY:	
Revenue Maximization				WHO: WHAT: WHEN: WHERE: WHY:	
Reduced Effectiveness of Competition				WHO: WHAT: WHEN: WHERE: WHY:	
Safety Improvements for Employees and Public				WHO: WHAT: WHEN: WHERE: WHY:	
Employee Effectiveness				WHO: WHAT: WHEN: WHERE: WHY:	

Figure 10.1 Commercial Risk Mitigation Worksheet.

of defects in the product—among product characteristics that the customer finds the most valuable. For an automobile manufacturer, it is vastly important that an automobile operate consistently day after day; that is the mark of quality for an automobile.

You do not have to use every business objective for your commercial risk mitigation plan. If you are working as a manager in a customer service call center, you may focus on the cost reduction category and the safety categories of risk mitigation. To assist in cost reduction, you could make employee training a higher focus and center training on how to resolve customer calls fully and quickly. Faster call resolution leads to each call center representative answering more calls, resulting in a higher level of efficiency and productivity. For safety, you may focus on using skid pads and frequent sweeping of walkways to prevent slips, trips, and falls and on using of a campaign of hand washing and cough covering to keep employees healthy. Safe and healthy employees reduce medical expenses and ensure a higher daily employee attendance rate. In these examples, you reduced risks specifically in your area of commercial operations that exposed the company to less risk.

Step 2: Identify the Primary Risks to the Business Objective

The second step of the commercial risk mitigation process is to identify the primary risks to the business objective. The competitive landscape for all businesses today is intense—from dry cleaners to global consumer electronics companies. All of these businesses face increasing consumer demands for better products at lower costs within an industry field that seems to possess more competitors on an almost daily basis. The business objective of reducing the effectiveness of the competition seeks to identify those areas where the competition is strong so that the company can plan steps to reduce the effectiveness of the competition.

The level of analysis to identify the primary business risks needs to be done at the level at which you see and experience the competition. For example, if you are the manager of a cellular telephone store, do not concern yourself with analyzing the research and development budget of your competition. Rather, understand the different cellphone plans and phone features of your two closest competitors and use that information to determine your competitor's greatest strengths. Once the strengths are identified, steps to mitigate those strengths can be identified and put in place. Using the business objective cost reduction example, you need to identify the areas of largest cost that you can successfully influence. You may not be able to influence the cost in monthly rent for a business location. However, you can do an analysis of the trends in utility costs of the store locations and, from that, determine ways to save cooling expenses, reduce garbage pickup costs, or find ways to recycle.

Step 3: Identify the Likelihood and the Severity of the Potential Risk

Step three revolves around identifying the likelihood of a risk occurring and identifying the likelihood of the severity of a risk event. The likelihood of a risk

Table 10.2 Commercial Risk-Mitigation Process and Risk Priority Planning Priority Table

Frequency	Severity	Total Impact
High	High	9
High	Medium	6
Medium	High	6
Medium	Medium	4
High	Low	3
Low	High	3
Medium	Low	2
Low	Medium	2
Low	Low	1

occurring is generally categorized into low, medium, and high likelihood. A low likelihood is something that occurs at most once or twice a year, a medium likelihood occurs once or twice every three months, and a high likelihood occurs once a month or more. This process to identify the frequency of a risk event occurrence is unscientific and general. You can add the precise statistics from company records or use a general assumption of the frequency of occurrence of the risk events.

The likelihood of the severity of a risk event is also evaluated on a low, medium, and high scale. The severity of risk events has to be grouped into categories based upon company specific data or your natural instinct and judgment on the grouping. The severity evaluation of low, medium, and high should describe the total cost to the business if the risk event happens. In the commercial risk mitigation process, there are often competing risks to be mitigated. You should come up with as many risks as possible per business objective that can have an influence and then identify both the likelihood and the severity of the risk event. The chart in Table 10.2 can be used to rank the risk events. The use of this chart will help you prioritize your risk mitigation efforts.

Step 4: Create the Risk Mitigation Plan

The final step in the commercial risk mitigation process is step four, the plan to implement the risk mitigation controls identified in step three. The plan to implement the risk mitigation steps needs to follow the military mission statement format. The military mission statement format is the following: Who is to perform the task? What task(s) are to be performed? When are the task(s) to be performed? Where are the task(s) to be performed? Why should the task(s) be performed with the expected outcome? The plan should only be specific enough to answer these five questions. It must also be simple and easy for multiple employees to perform, and it must ensure that employees can be trained efficiently, with a high degree of retention. It is essential that the risk mitigation plan be easy to implement. Figure 10.2 provides examples of a risk mitigation plan.

Risk Step	Risk Mitigation Step Detail	Example 1	Example 2
Industry		Light Manufacturing Factory	Company HQ Location
1	Business Objective	Safety of Employees	Cost Reduction
2	Primary Risk to the Business	Loss of worker productivity due to absence and medical costs due to slips, trips, and falls	Increasing costs to cool company headquarters
3	Likelihood of Risk Occurrence (low, medium, high)	Medium	High
	Severity of Risk Occurrence (low, medium, high)	Low	Low
	Risk Prevention Plan		
4	Who	2 employees assigned per schedule	Building maintenance engineer
	What	Sweep walkways, pick up trash in work areas, and mop up spills and water	Enforce window shades down in all windows, auto adjust building temp up when unoccupied
	When	Every 3 hours	Daily
	Where	All in use work areas and common walkways	All offices with windows and building temperature controls
	Why	Reduce hazards that cause slips, trips, and falls.	Reduce building solar heating and raise building temperature when unoccupied
Review	Success Criteria to Evaluate Effectiveness of Risk Mitigation Plan	Number of slips, trips, and falls per 100 employees prior to and after implementation of risk mitigation plan	Average monthly cooling cost before and after implementation of risk mitigation plan

Figure 10.2 Commercial Risk Mitigation Worksheet Example.

Assess the Effectiveness of the Risk Mitigation Measures

The conclusion of all risk mitigation efforts must be a regular review of progress or a lack of progress in meeting the business objectives. The first step in a progress review of risk mitigation is to have decided during the previous steps what measures of effectiveness or what success criteria would be used to evaluate the progress or lack of progress in the risk mitigation efforts. The use of a systematic measurement process is essential in determining whether the risk mitigation effort is successful, because, after all, if there are extensive cost reduction efforts but costs keep rising, the entire risk mitigation effort needs to be reviewed and a new plan implemented. Using the business objective of safety and an industry example of a manager for a trucking firm, a key business objective related to safety would be to reduce the frequency and severity of truck traffic accidents.

For this example, you would conduct prior research to determine a reasonable measure of risk mitigation effectiveness that reflects the whole business. For a trucking firm, the number of accidents per million miles driven and the average damage cost per traffic accident would be good pro-rated measures of effectiveness for the safety business objective. As a veteran manager, you would consistently track this safety measure of effectiveness as the firm implemented its safety risk mitigation efforts. If there was not an appreciable change, the safety risk mitigation efforts do not have to be completely abandoned, but they do have to be reviewed and a new safety risk mitigation plan placed into effect so the actual risk measure of traffic accidents per million miles can be reduced. It is essential that the risk mitigation efforts be managed and reviewed using data to ensure a plan's effectiveness. If a plan is in place, but it is not one that mitigates the risk, the entire risk management effort is suspect.

Summary

The following chart highlights two examples of risk mitigation in the business objectives of safety of employees and cost reduction. Again, risk mitigation efforts done well at the local level can have tremendous corporate savings and provide an excellent demonstration of leadership by example.

You play an essential role in ensuring the continuing success of the corporation by employing elements of the military risk management process to ensure that cost reduction, revenue generation, reduced effectiveness of the competition, safety of employees and the public, and employee effectiveness remain world-class—so that the business creates exceptional financial and operational results. Use the commercial risk mitigation worksheet to follow the steps of identifying the business objective, identify the primary risks to the business objective, identify actions to mitigate the risks, and create a plan to implement the risk mitigation steps as the path to help mitigate the company's operational and financial risks. At whatever level, from shop floor employee to CEO, every employee plays a role in helping mitigate risk for the company and the company's financial results.

SECTION 3

EXECUTE

Execute

Successful execution and the ability to carry out a plan successfully and meet the stated business objectives, in spite of the obstacles of the competition and the environment, is the true mark of a successful professional, military or business. Good execution requires not only a sound plan, but also the ability to apply sound leadership, team building, and sound management principles to successful execution. The characteristics of good execution utilize standard procedures so that routine processes are consistently executed well, use successive backup plans to ensure that the most important tasks are always done successfully, create and motivate teams so both the organization and individuals are successful, ensure that the plan remains on track in spite of a crisis or crises, and, if failure appears imminent, utilize a sound exit strategy to minimize loss.

CHAPTER 11

VETERAN LESSON 11: EMPLOY STANDARD OPERATING PROCEDURES (SOPs)

In the military, pre-mission inspection checks, rehearsals, serve as the foundation for mission preparation, ranging from a re-supply convoy to a combat raid. Why are these inspections so important? Because, just as in the manufacturing process for a television or computer, any type of variability that presents itself in the mission execution process is a potentially dangerous distracter from the accomplishment of the mission. Therefore, before performing a combat raid, all soldiers are checked for ammunition, water, and medical items; critical actions are rehearsed; and humane treatment of captured personnel are quadruply checked to ensure no mistakes. This same, constant, simple, and well-understood process can be applied to the opening procedures for a restaurant, factory-floor manufacturing operations, or the advance preparations for a sales call on an important customer—to ensure the highest possible quality execution and the lowest chance for a mistake. Just as in the military, in commercial operations, you want to reduce variability and risk to the lowest possible denominator to ensure the best chances for success.

Military Use of SOP

Military history provides a great example of the vital importance of SOPs in the Battle of 73 Easting during Gulf War I in 1991. During this ferocious tank battle, a mechanized company team (tanks and infantry fighting vehicles operating together) surprised an Iraqi Republican guard brigade during a sandstorm and, in a matter of minutes, completely reduced the effectiveness of the Iraqi brigade through devastating integrated direct firepower and close coordination of air and artillery supporting fires. Granted, the technology of U.S. weapons, night vision, and laser sights had a great deal to do with the victory, as did the element of surprise. However, the role of SOPs was an even greater element in the success of this engagement. The U.S. military units had drilled for months—indeed, some of the tank crews had been doing gun drills for years—in how to quickly identify, target, confirm target, fire, reload, and find the next target. This simple targeting SOP was the backbone of success for the Battle of 73 Easting. In each combat vehicle, the commander, vehicle driver, gunner, and loader all knew their tasks, had rehearsed their assigned tasks repeatedly, and knew precisely what needed to be done in a systematic fashion and in what sequence. SOPs, just as the military uses them in combat, are exceptionally valuable for businesses.

Business Use of SOPs

The business use of SOPs is also well understood. Anyone who has been to a McDonald's or other fast-food restaurant can well appreciate the vital importance of SOPs. From making Big Macs to store opening checklists to bathroom cleaning routines, McDonald's uses SOPs to ensure the quality of its food and employee performance to yield a uniform and satisfying customer experience. The business SOP performs many functions for the high performance of a business. Business SOPs help ensure uniform products and services, which promotes quality; purchasing SOPs help keep costs low; and business SOPs maintain and improve employee morale through enforcing common and high standards of performance. For many employees, the lack of a known and enforced standard creates a great deal of fear and uncertainty in their daily work lives. A business SOP is a reassuring tool for employees so they know precisely what is expected of them and what they can expect.

Business SOPs have a great deal of value for nearly every aspect of business operations. Variability in a business operation is one of the most damaging items to the success of a business operation. After all, how many trucks could Ford assemble in a day if all the doors were different sizes and the truck engine compartments did not fit the engines? Variability equals waste, and the role of the SOP is to stop variability in both company-centered activities, such as purchasing and safety, and customer-centered activities, such as customer service and product manufacturing.

The True Value of Business SOPs

The true value of business SOPs are best organized around the level of complexity of the task to be completed and how vital the task is to the customer. A businessperson can rightfully ask this question: If a task the company is doing does not directly or indirectly benefit the company, does the company really need to do it? Using the value of SOPs for the customer chart, there are four central areas of focus concerning how business SOPs help customers and help the business. The business SOPs are divided into four primary quadrants that have different levels of complexity and customer value. The breakout shown in Figure 11.1 is as follows:

Quadrant I: Low complexity and low customer value.
Example: The process used to pick up furniture outside of a store.
Quadrant II: High complexity and low customer value.
Example: The integration of all business functions for a company to reach low-
cost production.

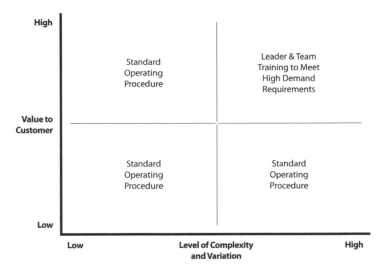

Figure 11.1 The Value of Commercial Standard Operating Procedures.

Quadrant III: Low complexity and high customer value.
Example: Clean food handling, storage, and preparation by a restaurant.
Quadrant IV: High complexity and high customer value.
Example: The design of a pickup truck engine and suspension system.

How Commercial SOPs Improve Business Success

High product and service satisfaction is the primary reason that customers remain with a company; the use of business SOPs for all functions in the respective quadrants is an essential step in retaining and meeting that level of customer satisfaction. Business SOPs help the company standardize both routine and highly complex operations that are of varying direct importance to the customer. This high level of standardization of routine processes through SOPs helps the company focus systematically on high quality, low cost, consistent innovation, and strong financial results. Business functions that fall within Quadrant IV, high complexity and high customer value, require customization for the customer and do not lend themselves to clear standardized procedures to meet all of the customer requirements. For example, the design of a wedding dress is a process that requires innovation, knowledge of fabrics, and extensive knowledge of fashion trends, and it is usually a once-in-a-lifetime customer purchase. The wedding dress example contains all Quadrant IV qualities, enormously complex and highly valuable to the customer. Quadrant IV products and services require a trained and integrated team to understand precisely all of the customer requirements and priorities in order to make the product to the customer specifications. The team working on a Quadrant IV product may employ SOPs in the subprocesses, but the overall project is individually tailored to the customer.

The Business SOP Creation Process

The process to create business SOPs is very similar to the process to create military SOPs. In short, the SOP creation process identifies the task to be completed, identifies what success looks like, assigns responsibilities for helping complete the task to all team members, rehearses and improves the SOP, implements the SOP into the business process, and looks for opportunities to review and improve the SOP periodically. The purpose of the SOP is to help the company promote quality, reduce cost, increase customer satisfaction, and improve financial results.

The Business SOP Creation Process

Step 1: Define the task, the purpose of the task, and how to measure its success.

Step 2: Create an SOP of who, what, when, and where to complete the task.

Step 3: Rehearse and revise the SOP to perfect who, what, when, where, and why to complete the task.

Step 4: Implement the SOP and incorporate it into operations and training.

Step 5: Schedule periodic SOP revision meetings (quarterly) to ensure that the SOPs are as effective as possible.

Your use of this process gives you a solid and repeatable framework to create business SOPs that allows your company to meet its business objectives in a safe, cost-effective, profitable, and efficient manner.

Step 1: Define the Task, the Purpose of the Task, and How to Measure Its Success

SOPs should only be created when the introduction of variability or conflicting standards will produce waste and lost opportunity for the business. Your first step is to identify the overall business task and purpose. This step in the SOP creation process also helps draw the appropriate fences around the business tasks so the SOP itself does not become too large and impossible to execute. The clear title in the task and its business purpose also helps members of the frontline staff understand why this SOP is important in the business process and that they play an important role in the company's success.

Equally important is how to measure the success of the SOP. In this way, there is a process to track the successful performance and adoption of the SOP and to determine whether the SOP is making a difference. Using the example of hotel room cleanliness, metrics such as customer surveys, inspection scores by local health officials, and hotel inspection scores by corporate representatives could all be used to track the overall effectiveness of the SOP. Equally, a metric signals when an SOP needs to be changed. If the SOP is being followed but the success measures associated with it are falling, the SOP itself needs to be reexamined, retrained, and reimplemented to ensure that it meets its base purpose. Finally, as a word of warning, companies should implement SOPs as their most important functions first and then work down the list in order of importance.

Step 2: Create an SOP of Who, What, When, Where, and Why to Complete the Task

Once the task for the SOP has been created, you need to create an initial draft plan of how the SOP will be implemented. The SOP plan creation process needs to be a team planning event. There are two ways to start the creation of a draft SOP. The first way to create a draft SOP is for you to conduct an individual time study on the process that the SOP is to address. You should do a systematic look at the current process and determine the following: Who is involved? What are they doing? When are they doing it? Where are they doing it? Why are they doing it? Naturally, this format is an extension of the military mission statement, and it provides a simple, easy-to-use format to identify what each person does along the way. Once you have accomplished this, you should gather the team that will perform the SOP, ask the members to share their initial findings, and use the team to confirm the findings.

The second way to assemble the draft SOP is to adjourn a team meeting and break the team into groups. Once the team is broken into smaller groups, direct each group to use the who, what, when, where, and why format to complete its respective, individual steps in the SOP process. Once the breakout teams have completed their work, the entire team reforms to share their results and assemble the draft SOP. You have to apply a great deal of soft, encouraging, and nondirective team leadership during this process to allow employee initiative and creativity in order to ensure a thorough, simple, and well-structured SOP.

The creation of the draft SOP process that identifies the who, what, when, where, and why for each team member is an evolutionary process. The team may go through two to four iterations of this process before a final and agreed-upon draft SOP is reached. The use of small rehearsals of the draft SOP is often an excellent idea to test the draft SOP. A quick rehearsal can often reveal problems or a good idea and help energize the team during the process. The team needs to look upon this process as a creative endeavor and not worry if a solution is not reached immediately. Some teams and individuals react best when they have an initial plan that they can adjust, as opposed to having to build one from scratch. Some teams like to approach a problem together from the ground level, in which case the use of breakout teams works best. In either case, use your best judgment to reach a solution. At the end of this step, the team has agreed upon a draft SOP that fully identified the who, what, when, where, and why in each step of the business SOP.

Step 3: Rehearse and Revise the SOP to Perfect Who, What, When, Where, and Why to Complete the Task

Once the draft SOP has been created and approved by the team, the team needs to schedule a series of full rehearsals or test implementations to ensure that the draft SOP is fully ready. The purpose of a rehearsal is a final test to ensure that the SOP covers all of the required steps to complete the task properly. The rehearsal of the SOP must include data gathering to ensure that the success metrics identified in step 1 can be gathered and demonstrate improvement.

The first part of the rehearsal process is to ensure that the team has sufficient baseline performance data on the existing process. The team should select a week in which the members perform the task for the SOP in the existing manner, track, and gather the success metrics identified in step 1. If a week's worth of data is not sufficient, a month's worth should be more than adequate. If the SOP is completed several times a day, a week should also be sufficient. This step of gathering baseline performance data is vital to the rehearsal process to ensure that the SOP that is implemented actually returns superior results to the existing performance metrics.

The next part of the rehearsal process is to implement the draft SOP. The team should plan for one to three days, or one to three weeks, to train and progressively improve its implementation of the new SOP. It will take workers time to integrate the new process into their daily tasks fully, as well as change learned patterns of behavior. The team should work slowly but efficiently to continue to build its proficiency with the draft SOP. Once everyone on the team is proficient in the new SOP, the team should have a week, or month, of full implementation of the new SOP and closely track the performance metrics.

Following the week or month of implementation of the new SOP, the team should meet again to compare the performance measures of the existing process vs. the performance measures of the new SOP. Did the SOP improve the process in terms of the success measures? Are people happy with the new process? Does it pass the "common-sense test?" If the process did not improve the measures, the team needs to decide whether more training on the new process is required or if the team members need to return to step 2 and create a new draft SOP. Examining the before and after results of the success metrics, as well as gauging the opinions of the team members, whether the new SOP works should be readily apparent. As a note of caution, you need to be proactive to make other employees comfortable with change, hear their concerns, and understand that the process of improving business process is evolutionary. The use of SOPs for core company and important customer processes is a key part of the execution processes.

Step 4: Implement the SOP and Incorporate It into Operations and Training

The implementation of the SOP is the most important step in the SOP creation process. Why? As you know, the actual implementation and use of an SOP is where the rubber finally meets the road—the business or unit actually starts to benefit from the implantation of the SOPs. The implementation of SOPs is just the first step in a sometimes long road of fully incorporating the SOP and its use into the company operations and company culture.

The success and use of SOPs for vital company and important customer processes must be fully communicated throughout the company. Within corporations, success must be celebrated and embraced by all members of the company. Leadership changes, departmental reorganizations, and product changes can all spell the end of a business task that is supported by SOPs. The celebration of

SOPs implementation and use, fully supported by the performance metrics defined in step 1, makes the corporation fully aware and appreciative of the SOP. Once the company appreciates and understands the value delivered by the use of SOPs, the company can move to expand the use of SOPs and incorporate SOPs into new employee training as well as employee refresher training.

Keeping the SOP process alive and fully functioning during personnel changes is a great challenge. The team that originally created and implemented the SOP remembers and understands the problems in the previous process and what was gained with the SOP. New personnel have no experience with the past, for better or for worse, and need to be trained on the reasons why the use of the SOP is so important. Furthermore, the use of success measures for all employees underscores how the business team measures and defines success. New personnel have to be trained in how to complete the SOP successfully and how to incorporate it into their daily workflows. More important, new personnel must understand the "why" of the SOP so they fully understand and appreciate its importance to the corporation's financial, product, and operational successes.

Step 5: Schedule Periodic SOP Revision Meetings to Ensure the SOPs Are as Effective as Possible

At least quarterly and, at a minimum, annually, the teams that created the SOPs need to reassemble and discuss ways to improve their business SOPs. The business world does not remain static for long, if at all. A review of the business success metrics, the reason and purpose of the task addressed by the SOP, and input from all members of the team about how the SOP is working will quickly bring to light whether the SOPs are still functioning in the best interests of the business.

The team must use both data and opinions to assess the performance of the business task. If the success measures say that the process is working well, but team and customer comments reveal a less than stellar performance, the team needs to revise step 1 to gather success metrics that fully reflect the performance of the product. The team may have to restart at step 1 to define the business task and success measures so the SOP continues to bring the company maximum value.

Summary

Variability in business operations produces waste, additional cost, and lost opportunity, which ultimately leads to a product or service that is not as appealing to customers as it could be. The use of the military SOP process was designed to apply a standardized way that soldiers would react and perform their duties in the highly variable conditions of the battlefield. SOPs in business can cover everything from how to open a new retail store to how to clean a hotel room properly to how to ensure the lowest cost that can be found for an item. The five-step process of how to create, integrate, and improve business SOPs is the way for you to reduce variability in your area of business operations and improve company financial results and operational effectiveness.

CHAPTER 12

VETERAN LESSON 12: BACK-UP PLANS TO ENSURE SUCCESS

As in the military, business is a process of creating and implementing business plans quickly and effectively in order to create a successful product or service. Most companies have annual, semiannual, and quarterly business planning processes, business assessment reviews, and other associated planning events to ensure that they make their volume, revenue, and profitability goals. However, the vast majority of businesses concentrate only on Plan A, and have only a marginal idea of what to do if Plan A does not work or does not work as effectively as planned.

Military Use of Back-Up and Contingency Plans

The military is an organization that comprises planners and executors. The military is driven by planning processes to bring the greatest amount of operational assets to the fight in the shortest amount of time possible. In addition to planning, all veterans realize that, a great deal of the time, military plans fail because of changes in the enemy, changes in orders, or changes in the environment. Therefore, the military Special Operations community uses a planning process, known as PACE, to ensure sufficient and robust back-up plans in order to accomplish the mission. The acronym PACE stands for "primary, alternate, contingency, and emergency" plans that are formulated for all critical mission tasks to ensure that the primary mission is a success.

You can use PACE in support of successful commercial opportunities in a variety of manners. For example, in ensuring the timely delivery of a part or service to a customer, the marketing and operations department may develop a PACE plan to ensure the customer receives the part on time and in proper condition. The PACE plan ensures the success of those critical functions that are vital to the success of the business. You can add significant value to the company's strategic and tactical business planning and execution process by incorporating back-up plans to ensure the business goals are achieved.

Reasons Business Plans Fail
without Back-Up Plans

So why do business and military plans fail? As a generalization, business and military plans fail for three primary reasons. The first reason why initial plans fail is that the competitive environment, that is the competition and how its operates in the market, changes in an unanticipated manner or a manner that calls for a complete readjustment of the plan. A classic business example of having to adapt a business plan to a sudden competitive change is when the manufacturers of portable compact disc (CD) players were confronted with the emergence of the Apple iPod portable music player. At the time of the emergence of the iPod, the portable CD players and their manufacturing companies were in a mature and stable market. Portable CD player manufacturers, such as Sony, were enjoying market success. However, in a matter of months, the portable CD player business model was turned on its head when a former noncompetitor, Apple, emerged with, essentially, a portable hard drive music player—to take away the personal portable music player market.

The second reason that initial business plans fail is a sudden, significant shift in the business environment or in society. Within the scope of the business environment is the industry, the macroeconomic business market, and the effects that the norms and behaviors of society exhibit upon consumers' and intended consumers' demand for your company's goods and services. An example of a sudden and dramatic shift in the business environment was the sudden reversal of consumer interest in large trucks and sport utility vehicles (SUV) beginning in 2007. The global automotive industry had a successful business model of producing large trucks and SUVs for the U.S. personal automobile market, a model that began in the late 1990s and continued for almost ten years. Starting in 2007 and amplifying the effects in early 2008, three factors began to shatter the existing automotive sales model. High gasoline prices, the unavailability of consumer credit, and a critically low consumer confidence index completely decimated the large vehicle market and severely damaged the financial health and overall vehicle sales of all automotive manufacturers.

The third and final reason that initial business plans fail is a reduction in the planned quantities of people, budget, equipment, and other assets, tangible and intangible, to support the successful execution of the business plan. Just as in the military, commercial assets comprising people, equipment, budget dollars, and other tangible resources, such as advertising support, customer service, and dedicated customer solution engineers, can be withdrawn and reallocated on, literally, a moment's notice. In early 2000, there were two primary companies competing for control of the customer relationship management (CRM) software marketplace, Siebel and Salesforce.com. CRM software is an innovative customer-activity tracking tool that can track sales win and loss rates, key customer contacts, frequency of customer orders, product pricing information, and provide in-depth analytics to support all customer profitability and customer assessment analysis. Siebel used a traditional software approach, in which purchased software is placed on organic company servers, but Salesforce.com used a lower cost and more innovative model to provide a "hosted" solution over the Internet. In the economic slowdown following the devastating attacks on 9/11/2001, Salesforce.com found itself competing against the CRM market leader, Siebel, and with a severely cut advertising and marketing budget as a result of the economy. However, Salesforce.com rallied and employed a small, direct, and inspired sales and advertising campaign in order to remain in business.

The PACE Back-Up Plan Creation Process

The acronym PACE stands for "primary, alternate, contingency, emergency"—representing a process that first establishes a priority plan to ensure the success of critical military and support functions. In the military, PACE is often used to ensure robust medical evacuation or ammunition re-supply plans—plans and process that have a critical, direct correlation to the success of a mission or operation. Indeed, PACE drives those functions whose success is essential to the

Table 12.1 The PACE Back-Up Planning Process Defined

Plan Category	Plan Against	Notes
P: Primary	Plan to employ all assigned assets against the competitor's most likely behavior under the existing market conditions.	This is your most likely plan based on the market, competition, and resources available
A: Alternate	The most threatening actions and changes in behavior by the primary competitor(s) that reduce the effectiveness of the primary plan.	This plan should account for the most dangerous steps your competitor(s) could employ.
C: Contingency	The worst case changes in the economy, current industry conditions, and societal trends that affect the primary business plan success.	This plan should account for the worst case changes in the market and customer preferences.
E: Emergency	The loss of significant assets to support the primary business plan and how the minimum assets can be used to best achieve the original plan's goals.	This plan should account for the loss of your most vital resources to implement the primary plan successfully.

success of a plan or operation. The organization of planning for the business event needs to employ a thorough and well-coordinated planning process for the primary business plan and then be supplemented by PACE back-up plans (see Table 12.1). The key point in the PACE planning process is to pre-formulate and anticipate, as best as possible, events that could go wrong or circumstances that could change in regard to the competition, the market conditions, and the resources available to achieve the business objective effectively.

PACE Planning Process: The Primary Plan

The primary plan of PACE represents the base or core business plan. The primary plan is the business's best estimate of what the competition will do, what the major market conditions that affect the plan will be, and the resources that have been assigned to the plan's execution and success. During the primary plan's preparation, it is vital that you clearly define the goals or success criteria. Examples of definitions include units sold, revenue achieved, profitability achieved, customer satisfaction scores, or stores opened. The use of precise and well-defined success criteria is important because, as the other plans for the alternate, contingency, and emergency events are formulated, they can be equally and fairly evaluated as to how well they meet the success criteria from the primary plan.

PACE Planning Process: The Alternate Plan

The alternate plan in PACE is to be used to adjust the plan to incorporate competitive changes that would make the primary competitor(s) choose their most dangerous strategy or course of action. An example of an alternate plan formulation was when Hewlett Packard (HP) was rebuilding its laptop market share in 2005 and 2006, following Mark Hurd's appointment as the new CEO. The global laptop market is extremely competitive and occupied by global technology leaders: Apple, Sony, Acer, Dell, Lenovo, and HP, to name only a few. While HP was trying to rebuild laptop market share, HP's competitors could have launched a price decrease or laptop bundling package to make the HP laptop more expensive than its direct competitors. Thus, HP had to have a competitive response prepared about how to respond quickly and effectively to a competitor's price actions so it could maintain its business objectives.

The methodology for determining the approach to the alternate plan is to identify the greatest vulnerabilities in the primary plan and then determine how the competition will exploit those plan weaknesses. For example, if the goals of the primary business plan is a new product launch, such as a new video game, the competition will most likely try to entice existing video game owners with discounted coupons for new video games, in order to make them loyal to their existing gaming device, as well as a way to bundle hot video game titles with new video game machine sales to keep the competition's video game device a strong seller. This use of discount coupons and product bundling would be a potential strong deterrent by the competition toward the company's sales of a new video game. The company's alternate plan would have to add plans to have a matching or doubling of the competitor's coupons, as well as a coupon program of its own to reduce or mitigate the new customer's incentive to purchase the competitor's video game. Additionally, the company would want to align itself with the next "hot" video game titles so that its video game machines were exclusively positioned (if possible) or if the company could be first in the new video game distribution. The company has to understand and articulate clearly what events trigger the implementation of the alternate plan. A good, well thought out, and coordinated alternate plan is a lifeline against a determined competitor.

PACE Planning Process: The Contingency Plan

Changes in the general society and macroeconomic condition are often the most devastating to a company's strategy because they are the farthest out of the company's direct span of control and ability to influence. For example, when the recession of 2008–2009 began in the summer of 2008, many companies that had, for years, enjoyed the ability to get their existing and potential customers access to low-cost lines of credit, that is bank loans, had their business operations nearly halted as the available lines of credit dried up. This lack of readily available and inexpensive consumer credit affected companies from automobile manufacturers to consumer electronic media to furniture sales. The contingency plans that these businesses would have required would revolve around securing several back-up credit providers to enable them to continue lending to their customers when their primary, alternate, and contingency (notice the trend in planning options!) sources were unable to meet their needs.

The methodology required for the contingency planning scenario requires the company to pair its primary plan against the largest macroeconomic, societal, and consumer points of influence that the business plan needs in order to succeed. For example, when large automobile sales began to slow because of the dynamic rise in gasoline prices, Toyota had a line of small, fuel efficient cars (i.e., the Yaris) and a line of hybrid cars (Prius, Camry, etc.) to provide to customers seeking a more fuel-efficient option. Toyota was still caught partially by surprise, but by having a contingency plan against macroeconomic and societal changes, it was the best able among all competitors to transition the business to meet the new consumer demand for fuel-efficient, stylish vehicles.

PACE Planning Process: The Emergency Plan

The loss of corporate resources to meet fully all of the planned goals of the primary plan is the rationale behind the emergency plan. The loss or reallocation of corporate resources prior to or during the implementation of a business plan can be a devastating offset to achieving a successful business plan. You need to treat the loss of dedicated business resources for the plan just as you would if you lost an asset assigned to you during a combat operation—continue the mission.

The methodology required to create a solid emergency plan for the loss of critical assets is to determine precisely what each asset was supposed to accomplish for the primary plan. The loss of assets takes extraordinary creativity to overcome the interruption to the plan and ensure the business plan is a success. For example, if your business plan to open a new store had its advertising budget reduced by 50%, you need to determine how the remaining 50% of advertising budget can accomplish 100% of the advertising goal. Creative thinking, involving everyone on your team, and initiative are absolute requirements to plan for a more creative use of business resources. Using the advertising example, you may need to look to local colleges and universities and collaborate with an advertising or creative arts class to get advice and advertising copy for the campaign. Additionally, when resources are reduced, you need to have a robust and effective assessment process so you can evaluate the effectiveness of the remaining assets. If the advertising budget was reduced, a likely alternative might be a more intensive use of direct mail advertising with a small coupon, so you can know precisely the usage and advertising effectiveness of the direct mail campaign. Emergency plans incorporate the loss of resources from the primary plan but maintain their absolute focus on accomplishing the original business objectives of the primary plan.

PACE Planning Process: Miscellaneous Items

Return to the Primary Plan for Adjustments

At the conclusion of the back-up plans for the alternate, contingency, and emergency events, the primary business planners and executors should return and modify the primary business plan with any key learning points. For example, while planning the emergency back-up plan to identify how to achieve as much of the plan as possible with the loss of key business resources, the business planners may have identified an important, new, more cost-effective way to achieve the plan. This learning point should be applied to the primary plan to make the primary business plan more cost-effective. In this way, the exercise of creating three types of back-up plans to deal with three potentially catastrophic events to the successful implementation of the business plan can lead to a strengthened and much improved primary business plan.

Combinations

There are innumerable potential combinations of both competitive, market, and resource changes that could affect the successful execution of the business plan and achieve the company goals for the project. By having pre-planned possibilities for changes in the competition, the market, and the resources available, the company executing the business plan has a ready bench of plans available. These pre-prepared contingency plans can then be combined and sorted to ensure that the contingency present matches the contingency plan prepared.

Summary

Successful business planning is more than just the alignment of people, assets, and resources within the existing market and competitive environments to meet a profitable, understood, and defined customer need. Good business planning has to understand quickly and effectively how to modify the business plan to reach as much as possible of the original business goal. The military planning process, or PACE, helps a company anticipate what changes need to be applied to the original business plan when the competitive environment changes, the alternate plan; when the market and customer conditions change, the contingency plan; and when the resources available to support the plan change, the emergency plan. Nearly anyone can plan for success. As a successful veteran business planner, you plan a great primary plan but then support the primary plan with alternate, contingency, and emergency plans so that as much of the original plan's goals can be achieved. A business plan, unless it is a flexible tool that anticipates changes, will not be worth a penny after the first competitive and marketplace "salvos" are fired. Good business planning supports achieving the commercial mission, no matter what the changes in the competitive landscape, the greater economy, and the internal company resources assigned may be.

CHAPTER 13

VETERAN LESSON 13: CREATE AND LEAD POWERFUL TEAMS

The creation of a true team is one of the greatest assets you can bring to a commercial organization. Good teams are focused on their missions, have an atmosphere of mutual support, foster a healthy climate of respect and support, challenge other members of the team to improve, focus on helping others learn vital skills, and have a passion to complete the mission to the highest level of quality achievable. The ability to lead teams in an agile manner through a land-scape of sudden change and conflict between business functions, customers, and market trends is a unique ability that, as veterans, you possess and that corporations require.

The Need for Dynamic, Focused Leadership in a Complex Business World

Leadership is the practice of directing, motivating, and shaping a group or groups of individuals to work together to accomplish a set or series of goals in an ever-improving manner over time. Leadership, in its most fundamental form, is making people maximize their individual contributions toward the greater good, which is directed toward the goal of the group. Military leadership teaches leaders to become innovative, open to new ideas, and how to form and lead teams to success in apparent indifference to the obstacles confronting them. Military and business organizations are both faced with a constant need for leaders who can focus, motivate, teach, and lead groups of people through difficult problems.

A special forces officer, leading an "A" team to clear a building of terrorists, and a CEO, launching a new product in a competitive marketplace, face vastly different leadership challenges. Both of these challenges require driven, dynamic, inventive, and focused leaders to bring success to their organizations. The leaders in both of these situations require that the leaders direct, motivate, and shape the groups of individuals they lead to accomplish their assigned tasks. The leadership style that two leaders employ varies greatly, depending on the environment, urgency, importance, and risk required for meeting the group's goal. When General Douglas MacArthur proposed and led the Inchon landings that reversed the failing course of the Korean War in 1950, he used an extremely directive leadership style that was both a hallmark of his leadership and one of his downfalls. Bill Gates, an individual who is equally driven, for the use of computers to solve personal, business and societal problems, used a collaborative style, intermixed with exceptional focus and charisma, to make Microsoft a global powerhouse of computing. Both MacArthur and Gates were successful, and both employed vastly different leadership styles. Leaders use the leadership style—directive, collaborative, or a combination—that they think can best lead their team to accomplish the mission.

A leader must combine dynamic driven leadership with the proper managerial techniques in order to create a business organization that is fundamentally sound, competitive, and viable for its customer base. No amount of dynamic leadership will overcome the deficit of failures in accounting, a deep knowledge of customers, or quality manufacturing, to name only a few. Likewise, an organization that is well managed but lacks drive, motivation, and winning spirit will never succeed in a competitive marketplace. The net result of proper leadership styles and effective managerial methods is an organization that can plan, adapt, and win in the marketplace in an ethical fashion, meet customer expectations, and remain ahead of the competition. Business leaders must employ their most effective leadership styles and methods to ensure that they motivate and direct employees to utilize the most effective managerial techniques to solve their organization's resource utilization challenges.

Team Leadership Demands Perfection and Delivers Great Results

Military team leadership is a demanding task. Excelling in the global business arena requires skill sets similar to those of a military leader. Business leaders, like military leaders studying and understanding enemy soldiers on an objective, must be skilled at understanding the competitive environment and creating organizations that excel, adapt, and renew themselves as the competitive environment evolves. Business leaders must be able to read intricately what customers want, understand the direct and indirect competition, and know how to run a fluid, synchronized, cost-effective organization.

Business leaders must be adept at putting together teams where none have existed before, able to lead those teams, and able to understand different language, organizational, technological, business value, and cross-cultural issues. Military leadership emphasizes focused leadership, a focus on ethics and values, leadership by example, and decentralized execution. Business leaders need to create organizations that respond rapidly to changing market conditions, unexpected advances by the competition, and a rapidly changing workforce so their organizations remain successful. Finally, effective team leadership is more about managing for the day and for the current project. Effective team leadership is creating, fostering, and maintaining an atmosphere of trust, results, continuous improvement, and personal initiative that leads to superior business results and great products and services for customers.

There are four steps for you to build and maintain effective teams in commercial organizations.

Step 1. Establish and communicate a strategic vision.
Step 2. Collaborate with the team to create a winning plan.
Step 3. Praise publicly, develop employees privately, and seek feedback from all.
Step 4. Develop others as leaders for their career success.

Step 1: Establish and Communicate a Strategic Vision

Leaders are trained to develop, execute, and assess their strategy constantly in a continuous and constant loop. The clear strategic direction of an organization is vital for business leaders to establish so they can clearly and seamlessly integrate their strategic plan with the actions of all members of their business unit. The formulation of good business strategies is not a systematic or major problem in business today. Business school curriculums, strategy consultants, strategic planning groups, and industry experts are all primary players in strategy formulation.

A problem for business today is how effectively leaders communicate that strategy to their employees and other team members. A leader can have a grand business plan of product introductions, quality improvements, and new customer acquisitions. The challenge remains of how that business leader translates the strategy for the person in aisle 4, cube 8, so that he or she is motivated, feels like a contributing member of the team, and is looking to do everything that can be done to ensure that his or her part of the strategy is a success. The true strategic experts are those who not only get the business strategy right, they are also the ones who effectively communicate, include, challenge, and reward members of their team as they execute and revise the strategy into a successful business venture.

The communication of the business strategy has to be frequent, use both formal and informal methods, be understandable by employees at all levels, and help provide context and direction to the execution of the strategy. The communication frequency of the strategic direction and the strategic progress should be anywhere from weekly to monthly, at a minimum. These strategic communication sessions should follow a similar format that shows the weekly and monthly progression in the success metrics of the strategy. The use of customer comments, articles, or quotes from the business media and trade media and special recognition of individuals who executed their portion of the strategy particularly well should be recognized in front of the team. Finally, the leaders should highlight important next steps in the progression of the business strategy. These meetings do not have to be long—30 minutes or less are acceptable. The use of this frequency and format helps ensure that everyone within the organization understands how the strategy is proceeding and knows what to expect in the immediate future.

The formality of strategy meetings can be similar to the formal meeting previously described, or it can be as simple as a meeting around the coffee pot on a Tuesday at 10 AM. Formal approaches are well used to put out a lot of information in a regular format and help the entire team understand the full progress. An informal approach—say, employing "management by walking around"—helps the leader understand and fully engage the entire team's understanding and progress of the strategy, as well as address any private concerns or questions that individual team members may have. "Management by walking around" (MBWA) is a concept originated by Tom Peters wherein the business leader walks casually through an organization, stops, talks with employees, and learns what is actually happening in the organization. The use of frequent commander visits to combat zones is an excellent example of MBWA so a leader discovers precisely what is happening. The formal communication process is great for telling the story, but the informal approach to individuals or small groups is vital to get employees to believe how the strategy is progressing.

The final two areas focus on the understandability of the strategic updates and the ability for those updates to provide context and direction. The success metrics of the strategy should be clear, simple, and understandable to any employee. Every employee likes to know how the company's or business unit's strategy is progressing, as well as what areas need to be improved—simple, clear metrics allow employees to do this. The metrics should also be able to instruct in simple, clear terms what employees need to do or continue to do in order to make the strategy a success. The purpose of simple, clear, understandable success metrics is to encourage action and initiative among all employees so that each person can be an active participant in the execution of the strategy. The ability of a leader to publicly update and communicate the progress of a strategic business execution is an incredibly powerful morale builder. Employees are inspired when they know the plan, how the plan is doing, when they have a leader who seeks their individual input, and when strategic updates inspire them to individual action and initiative.

Step 2: Collaborate with the Team to Create a Winning Plan

A great business strategist not only creates a good plan and communicates it well and frequently, he or she knows that generating input from all employees to the plan and its subsequent execution creates an even better plan. Teams that collaborate honestly, openly, frequently, and universally create an even better plan and ensure a successful execution, even when conditions and the environment change. Leaders that allow, encourage, and support individual employee initiative into the planning and execution process almost automatically create employee support, excitement, and "buy in" for the business plan. An employee who has had input into a business plan is much more engaged and ready to support the business plan and its execution. Involvement in the planning means a much greater chance of success for the plan's execution.

You need to have a structured approach to the business planning process that encourages active employee participation but also provides a structure to help employees do their best to add input to the business plan and its execution. The business leader must provide initial scope to the project so team members understand the macro business goals and objectives and what the company is attempting to achieve. Furthermore, the business leader should also outline competitive threats as well as industry trends so team members understand the full context of their efforts.

The use of technology is crucial in allowing regular, systematic feedback to the business leader. Leaders can create blog sites that allow their plans to be posted and then encourage employee feedback. Leaders can also use online surveys and town hall-style meeting sessions to survey, gather, and dissect employee feedback and gauge employee morale and motivation on the likelihood of the plan's success.

Step 3: Praise Publicly, Develop Employees Privately, and Seek Feedback from All

Leaders also have an obligation to develop the skill sets and improve the quality of work of their team members. All teams and their leaders must maintain a strong and diligent focus on the development of their team members. The professional development of team members accomplishes dual goals for the corporation: the company improves in its performance because employees are more competent, and employee morale improves because employees feel more valued and regarded by the company. Win-win situations in business are rare, but the development of team members is one of those unique win-win situations where everyone truly does win.

Praise and compliments are a vital part of good team leadership. Praise by itself should be used rarely. Why? Praise of and by itself can send confusing and contradictory signals that may make the employee feel less valued. For example, if my manager walks by and says, "Great job! Keep it up!" I wonder whether I am being praised for the latest deal I closed, a subordinate of mine who was promoted, or how I parked my car this morning. Praise and compliments, to be truly effective in reinforcing and promoting optimal performance, must be timely, specific, personal, and genuinely delivered. Leaders must offer praise for a good deed quickly, they must highlight what was done correctly, and the praise must be delivered in a manner that conveys genuine respect and appreciation for the action. Using this format, a leader uses praise as a tool to reinforce positive performance. A leader must always use judicious praise in a public setting that helps reinforce a positive action to a group. In a commercial setting, promotions, public recognition, and increases in salary and benefits are the most effective ways to improve performance.

By far the hardest part of team leadership—but also the most rewarding—is the development and motivation of employees who can improve their performance. Employee development is one of the most vital tasks of a team leader. Employee development is a task that is best approached from an oblique angle that allows employees to identify areas that they need to improve, offers concrete recommendations about how they can improve, and then sets a timetable and work plan to improve their performance. Employee development must never "attack" an employee's performance head-on and in a group setting. Employees can be praised publicly, but employees must be developed in private so they can ask questions, understand the feedback, and voice their concerns in an atmosphere that does not make them look incompetent in front of their peers.

In the development session, the team leader and the employee should have a pre-arranged meeting in a private, yet public, setting to discuss the employee's performance. The team leader should help employees identify what they do well and what they can improve in comparison to the expectations of the company. Once the item that the employee needs to improve has been identified, the team leader needs to focus on concrete, definable, and actionable items that the employee can do to improve. The team leader needs to provide resources, training, time, and motivation to ensure that the employee has all of the required resources to correct the deficiency.

The final action for a team leader is to meet regularly with team members, as a group and as individuals, to receive feedback. The team leader should receive feedback both on the business performance and on strategy. The team leader must also create an environment that allows team members to offer leadership performance feedback and improvement suggestions. The ability of a leader to gather good performance feedback from the team is built entirely on an atmosphere of mutual respect, concern, and development of team members. A leader who seeks to promote, develop, and improve team members sees those same team members return the efforts to the team leader. However, leaders who ignore their team members or take them for granted create a significant amount of risk in developing a positive, honest, and mutually supporting relationship with their team.

Step 4: Develop Others as Leaders for Their Career Success

The final obligation that leaders have is to improve the leadership skills and leadership capabilities of their team members. A team leader makes a company and an organization great by helping grow leaders within the organization. The personal skills development concepts, identified in step 3 of this chapter, are the first critical elements that team leaders can implement to help team members improve their leadership skills. Good leaders have solid skill sets, and coaching helps ensure that development.

The leadership development that team leaders can perform revolves around creating leadership opportunities for team members within their organization and then allowing those team members to receive executive visibility for their efforts. The leadership development opportunity should be a smaller project that is difficult yet achievable for the leadership candidate to perform. It is critical that the leadership project not be too easy or too difficult. A project that is too difficult unnecessarily discourages, and a project that is too easy fails to motivate and does not develop the necessary leadership skill sets. The leadership project must be well defined, adequately resourced, supported by other team members, and have a duration of one to three months. The leadership candidate in charge of the project must be allowed to plan, structure, and execute the project to a successful conclusion.

The team leader should schedule a weekly project check-in with leadership candidates to verify their plan, ensure progress, answer questions, and gauge how well the leadership candidates are performing in the team they are leading. Additionally, leadership assessment tools, such as 360-degree interviews and other feedback tools, allow the team leader and the leadership candidate to have honest and critical feedback to improve their leadership style. The weekly leader check-in is essential to further develop the leadership candidate's skill sets, as well as keep the plan on track. The overall goal is to stretch, coach, and develop leadership candidates so they have a success, but not to make it so easy that it is a "gimme."

One of the leadership methods used in a small team is to have a revolving "super project" that the entire team identifies as a problem and then a team member volunteers to lead the project. Each team member is required to lead a super project at least two or three times annually. This method allows team members to exercise a great deal of initiative among themselves, identify a set of possible projects, chose a project through internal consensus, and have a team member lead a project to its successful conclusion. Throughout this project, stay on the sidelines and coach the leadership candidates on their leadership style and project management plan. The coaching concept is to keep the plan on track, but also to allow leadership candidates enough "slack" to get into problems and then solve them—the task of all leaders.

The final benefit of developing new leaders within the team is that it creates a business succession plan within the team. No leader likes the concept of no promotions. Team leaders must grow leaders within their team so they have ready replacements when a promotion opportunity presents itself. The growing and development of internal team leaders also presents a great opportunity for leaders to position individuals trained by them within the company and the industry. The true benefit of growing leaders within a team is that it makes the team stronger, improves the existing team leader's ability to coach and teach, and establishes a ready pool of leaders for the company to use.

Summary

Creating a well-functioning business team is only one aspect of the team leadership dynamic for good business results. Business leaders must communicate frequently, clearly, consistently, and in a variety of formats and settings so they not only inform employees of the strategic plan but also inform them of strategic progress. Leaders not only inform and seek feedback, but they also encourage employee input into the strategic plan, its execution, and the assessment of the plan's progress. Employees, to be good team members, must be lead in a fashion that allows them to express themselves and provide input for their opinions on how to operate the business successfully.

In addition to employee feedback, business leaders need to ensure they develop other employees into future leaders, employing a constructive coaching format that not only improves employee performance but also creates a generation of future leaders for the business. Finally, a team functions within an atmosphere of honesty, openness, initiative, self-improvement, coaching, involvement, and feedback. This creates a working environment where the input of every member of the team is valuable, and every member of the team seeks to improve so they can, in turn, produce better business results. Great teams are difficult to create and maintain, but the reward is unsurpassed business results, more fulfilled and motivated employees, and new leaders for the corporation—a result worthy of the endeavor.

CHAPTER 14

VETERAN LESSON 14: USE MILITARY CRISIS-MANAGEMENT TECHNIQUES

Crisis-management skills are an expertise and proficiency that very few commercial employees bring to the business world. Those commercial and nonprofit employees who thrive in crisis—fire fighters, smoke jumpers, police, financial bond traders, and crisis-management experts—all possess the same cool characteristics of military personnel when it comes to meeting a crisis head-on, solving the crisis, and getting back to business quickly. As veterans from the recent combat operations in Iraq, Afghanistan, and elsewhere in the globe, you are experts in seeing through the initial crisis, keeping a cool head, maintaining a focus on the most important items, meeting the crisis head-on to solve it, and then getting back to the mission. A crisis is rarely the mission of an organization, but a crisis is always a mission distraction for any organization. The goal of a crisis is to identify it quickly, solve it, and get back to the primary mission at hand.

Corporate Crisis Management

Crisis management for commercial organizations is keeping the company on its business and mission track in spite of severe events that threaten the core stability of the corporation and its business model. A crisis for a corporation very often threatens the very existence of the company, and a corporate crisis can come from areas where the company is least likely to expect an attack. A crisis can be a failure in product design or testing that leads to customer injuries, a devastating weather event, or a rapid change in the market structure and consumer preferences that leave the corporation scrambling for its financial life.

One of the best examples of corporate crisis management is the Tylenol capsule product-tampering scare. In 1982, in metro area Chicago, there were a series of deaths from cyanide poisoning caused by illegal product tampering of Johnson and Johnson's Tylenol capsule product. In a stellar example of corporate crisis management, Johnson and Johnson responded quickly and forcefully to remove products from the shelves, created safer product packaging, communicated aggressively with the public about the crisis and about steps to keep safe, and led the over-the-counter pharmaceutical industry in developing new product packaging safety standards. Successful corporate crisis management is characterized by the following principles: (1) identification that a crisis is occurring, (2) an open leadership and communication approach for company employees and the public, (3) a confident, humble demeanor by management, and (4) anticipation of follow-on crisis events and solid execution of crisis mitigation steps.

Military Crisis Management in Action

The Allied airborne forces, employing both parachute and glider forces, rehearsed their separate operations for months prior to the Normandy landings during World War II. However, on the climactic night for the operation, June 5 and the morning of June 6, 1944, chaos and crisis ensued. There were navigation errors, equipment malfunctions, unmarked drop zones and landing zones, and unanticipated Nazi German military action, resulting in massive numbers of miss-drops of parachute and glider forces. Any airborne or air assault soldier knows that when you get dropped at night, in combat, and in unfamiliar ground, there is a crisis if you do not land on or near the correct drop zone or landing zone. One of the great, amazing, and unanticipated results of the miss-dropped Allied airborne landings was how key leaders, understanding their mission statement, commander's intent, and concept of the operation, were able to reorganize quickly and effectively on the ground, form ad-hoc units, and still adequately accomplish the Allied airborne mission sets, despite a significant disruption to the original plan. The crisis of the miss-drops and wrong landing zones was only a temporary distraction to the Allied mission goals. The Allied military forces involved reorganized themselves, solved the crisis of incorrect landings, and resumed their original operations to accomplish the mission.

The Steps of Military-to-Business Crisis Management

There are four major steps in the military-to-business crisis management process. This is not intended to be an exhaustive list, rather a focus on key principles for crisis management. The four principles of military-to-business crisis management are as follows:

> Step 1: Identify that a crisis is occurring.
> Step 2: Employ an open leadership and communication style.
> Step 3: Maintain a confident and humble demeanor.
> Step 4: Anticipate follow-on crisis events and ensure solid execution of crisis mit-
> igation steps.

The use of these four principles ensures that the corporation has the best chance to emerge through the crisis with as little damage as possible.

Step 1: Identify That a Crisis Is Occurring

This seems like a simple matter, but how do you know that a crisis is occurring? In the military, a crisis usually occurs when there is an unexpected enemy attack or the loss of a critical resource or capability that requires a major reworking of a plan or operation. In business, there are seldom the telling symbols that a crisis is occurring—such as the crash of artillery, the enemy occupying new ground, or an enemy attack, or the appearance of a new weapon system. For a business, the most important strategic item to have is a dashboard that reflects, as accurately as possible, the day-to-day operations of the business. In business, there are two general tools used to monitor the health of the business: the scorecard and the dashboard. The scorecard is essentially a "report card" of how well the business is doing over time; it looks backward over months and years to compare changes in customers, revenue, product mix, profitability, and costs, to name only a few. In contrast to the scorecard, the dashboard is a near real-time tool that attempts to see an immediate change in the business that requires management's attention.

Dell uses monthly revenue of computers sold and cost per unit sold as scorecard items to monitor its business operations and overall financial health. Dell also uses the number of computers sold by mid-morning as a dashboard item to predict any problems in demand or to determine whether Dell needs to offer more advertising or a short-term promotion as a way to get business back to target levels. Dell uses units sold and revenue both as a scorecard and a dashboard item. However, it is the units sold by mid-morning as a dashboard item that point to any immediate cause for a crisis in a business.

Your role in your business is to identify and help construct those dashboard items, usually no more than two to three, which serve as immediate or early indicators if the business or business plan is moving into a crisis. For most businesses, the daily sales rate, the daily average price per unit sold, or daily or hourly foot traffic numbers per retail store all serve as dashboard items if their business is entering or is in a crisis. A scorecard can have 20, 30, or even 100 different items that different business functions or various executives in the business look at to see if the business is functioning correctly. The dashboard items that signal a crisis, a looming crisis, or a potential crisis should be common to all business functions and should be easily understandable by all. The types of indicators for a dashboard are unique to every business. The immediately relevant task for you is to find, understand, and reach internal consensus on what those dashboard indicators are, how they are defined, how they are gathered, and how they are communicated throughout the organization so everyone can track and see if there is a crisis.

Step 2: Employ an Open Leadership and Communication Style

The next most important item to the identification of a crisis is the management style that the senior executive team members adopt before they are in a crisis and once they are in a crisis. You realize that, in a crisis, soldiers and all people literally crave leadership. There are two difficult aspects of a crisis for the company's employees: (1) not knowing what is going on, and (2) not being told what you can do to help solve the crisis. When employees either do not know what is going on during a crisis or what they can do to help solve or mitigate the crisis, at best, chaos ensues, or, at worst, nothing happens. This applies equally to employees, customers, suppliers, the public, government officials, and other interested parties. All groups want to have open communication so they know what is going on. Nothing happening is the worst thing to occur in a crisis, because no action or the inability to act is devastating in a crisis—literally the "deer in the headlights."

An open leadership style by all management levels is essential to help the corporation navigate through the crisis. An open leadership style is defined as one that uses inclusive leadership techniques to help gather feedback concerning the crisis solution(s) from all employees and uses a direct, open, frequent, and nonthreatening communication style to let everyone know what has happened, what is happening, and what the company plans to do next. Open leadership before a crisis also helps the corporate executives identify early on that a crisis is taking place or will happen—because employees, customers, government officials, and the media are more relaxed and comfortable, knowing that they will be heard and their opinions considered.

The final element to an open leadership style in a crisis is an open communication style with employees, customers, suppliers, the public, government officials, and other interested parties. All of these groups, from employees to other interested groups, have a stake and an important role in the successful operation of the corporation. The best type of communication style is open and frequent—one that allows the media, customers, and suppliers to ask questions and receive information. The frequent use of these communication sessions allows the corporation's management team members to demonstrate what they are doing to solve the problem, ask for assistance if it is needed, and demonstrate that they are fully in control of the crisis, the response to the crisis, and its successful resolution. Finally, frequent and open communication sessions allow the company to have an "open door" approach to the crisis resolution and show that it is doing everything in its power to resolve the problems.

This type of open leadership and communication style is extraordinarily difficult to do under times of crisis: this leadership style requires a great deal of time, and the news cycle moves at an ever-faster rate. The corporate leader can leverage technology, such as e-mail, voice mails, Web-based town hall meetings, and the like, to get their message out in a timely, accurate, and frequent fashion. Additionally, by limiting the use of closed door meetings around employees, they can much more positively promote an atmosphere of trust, confidence, and solution-oriented behavior of employees. There is no substitute for the open leadership and communication style in a crisis.

Step 3: Maintain a Confident and Humble Demeanor

During the darkest days of the recession of 2008–2009, the leaders of the U.S.-based auto manufacturers came to a committee hearing of the U.S. Congress in November 2008, to make their case on how a U.S.-funded temporary capital infusion would make their companies more financially stable. Despite a solid presentation and a willingness to listen, they were almost summarily turned away from the Capitol and Congress. Their crime was taking private airplanes to the congressional meetings in Washington, DC. No one can fault the auto executives for their time management, efficiency, or the use of an asset that their company owned. What the use of private aircraft by these executives signaled was the lack of a humble demeanor. In a crisis, a leader must appear humble, confident, and hard working in order to project an aura of quiet confidence that people want to work. Special forces officers who worked among "A" teams appeared almost bored or unconcerned, even though they may have been equally terrified or unsure inside. No one wants a scared or unsure leader. Quiet confidence and a "can do" attitude by a leader are absolute requirements for successful resolution of the crisis.

People want to see and be considered by their leader in a time of crisis. During the June 6, 1944, D-Day landings, the situation on Utah beach was becoming increasingly ominous. A foundering U.S. attack, ineffective landing beach operations, and an effective Nazi German defense all made for a dire situation. Brigadier General (BG) Theodore Roosevelt, Jr., was present on the beach during the landings and was a stellar example of a confident and humble leader under exceptionally demanding battlefield conditions. BG Roosevelt moved confidently and openly among the stalled invasion force to direct, inspire, and order the U.S. forces to resume the attack and move inland. BG Roosevelt's actions are widely credited for making the actions on Utah beach a success.

Step 4: Anticipate Follow-On Crisis Events and Ensure Solid Execution of Crisis Mitigation Steps

The final step in business crisis management is to anticipate follow-on crisis events and ensure that there is an exceptional execution of the crisis mitigation plan. A crisis can be bad for business operations, but the spiraling effect of subsequent follow-on effects initiated by the initial crisis can be devastating. During the clean-up and initial response to the devastating humanitarian crisis in New Orleans and the surrounding areas caused by hurricane Katrina, Lieutenant General (LTG) Russel Honoré emerged as a leader keen on anticipating the effects of the crisis and executing solid crisis execution measures. In his response to the growing humanitarian disaster in New Orleans and surrounding areas, Honoré was unconcerned with blaming other parties. Honoré was solely interested in getting everyone moving in the right direction, with the right attitude, and with the right supplies to start making a difference for all people in the disaster-affected area. Honoré knew that the crisis and its response would be defined by the follow-up and the ability to get effective aid to people quickly. The response by the U.S. military to the hurricane Katrina disaster was a great example of how organizations need to predict follow-on crisis events and then aggressively execute crisis mitigation plans.

The central point of step 4 for you is not to become too focused on the immediate crisis, but to be proactive and employ initiative to anticipate follow-on crisis events, create a crisis mitigation plan, and ensure a solid execution of the crisis mitigation plan. You can employ all of the planning, leadership, and risk management tools from this book to help predict the follow-on crisis events and the execution required to complete the crisis mitigation steps successfully. Crisis planning and crisis action plan execution need to be carefully weighed and addressed so the areas with the greatest criticality to affect the success of the business are targeted first. The crisis mitigation planning must focus fully on addressing, in a descending criticality, the items that most threaten the success of the business. Items such as the synchronization matrix, P-A-C-E back-up plans, and risk management techniques are especially helpful in formulating a solid crisis mitigation execution plan. Finally, the execution of the crisis mitigation plan is the most important part. Spend 30% of the time planning but 70% of the time preparing and executing.

Summary

Successful military-to-business crisis management is characterized by the following principles: (1) identification that a crisis is occurring; (2) an open leadership and communication approach for company employees and the public; (3) a confident, humble demeanor by management; and (4) anticipation of follow-on crisis events and solid execution of crisis mitigation steps. Crisis management is as much art as it is science. There is no formulaic approach to prove that a teaspoon of openness, three media briefings a day, and two back-up plans for a factory's power source will yield successful management of a crisis. However, by adhering to the military-to-business crisis management steps, you will be in a much better position to master the crisis, mitigate the effects of the crisis, and ensure that the business remains on track.

CHAPTER 15

VETERAN LESSON 15: PREPARE AN EXIT STRATEGY

Military planners have long understood the vital necessity of contingency and multiple contingency plans in case an operation is not successful. At times, all military operations have had to include a retreat or withdrawal of forces when the attack or defense would not be a success. During the Korean War, planners for the U.S. Army's X Corps developed multiple sea re-deployment plans to allow U.S. Army and U.S. Marine Corps units, fighting their way out of North Korea around the Chosin Reservoir, to escape almost overwhelming attacks by Chinese Communist Forces.[1] Even though U.S. military forces were in the midst of a successful month-long offensive operation, they quickly developed a strategy to exit successfully. This strategic exit plan allowed the U.S. military to preserve its combat forces to fight another day, as they quickly adapted their strategy from the offensive to the defensive. The U.S. Army X Corps command and staff saved thousands of lives and essential military equipment during a disheartening retreat, because they were able to adapt quickly to the requirements of a new strategic direction—forced onto them by the Chinese invasion, dwindling supplies, and exceptionally cold weather.

The Critical Business Value of Exit Strategy Planning and Execution

Business strategies and personal career plans often require the formulation of an exit strategy to ensure the core business or personal career remains successful and continues to advance when faced with unexpected adversity. In the mid-1990s, IBM had to make the strategic decision from writing operating systems for personal computers (PCs) as Microsoft established its dominance in the area of PC operating systems. However, IBM, by leaving a fruitless effort in PC operating systems, was able to redirect resources to a much more successful enterprise built on business systems, network integration, and consulting. Indeed, the ability to exit a strategic position quickly, effectively, and efficiently should be viewed as a corporate strength and not a weakness.

From the perspective of personal career management, in a corporation, the path to promotion and advancement is more likely to be nonlinear than the linear or stair-step career advancement of military careers. Your understanding when you have to exit a career direction and adapt your career plans is essential. You have to maintain your own career exit strategies and strategic career change adaptations for your career development. Furthermore, you must decide if, when, and under what conditions to change your employer, industry, or career functional area. All good business and career development strategies have both entrance and exit components to ensure success. Failure comes when a company or individual misses or refuses to recognize when it needs to adapt its strategy to avoid failure. Moreover, if that strategic business adaptation is unsuccessful, the firm must determine when and how to exit its current business strategy and reallocate those resources to a more successful business project.

Initial Actions in the Creation of an Exit Strategy

The initial creation of an exit strategy serves two roles. First, it provides vital input to create a preventative strategic plan to avert or reduce the likelihood of a failure of the business plan. Second, it helps the business agree on an end point or a "line in the sand"—a point at which the business will no longer invest resources into a failed strategy—and then redirect those resources to a more successful project. To dispel an immediate impression, the creation of an exit strategy and the defining of exit conditions do not mean that a business team is planning to fail or is afraid to take significant risk in a business venture. Rather, the creation, analysis, and discussion of exit strategies and exit scenarios will better help the corporation understand where it has risk, why it has risk, and how to implement preventative measures to ensure the success of the business plan prior to the implementation of an exit plan for a business strategy. Finally, the creation of an exit strategy and various exit scenarios is not a purely scientific methodology that yields an answer or business plan forecast with absolute precision. The use of scenario planning is an inherently unscientific method, but it is a quick, efficient, and thorough method that reveals risks and good countermeasures.

Commercial Exit Strategy Process Steps

The insightful analysis, description, and forethought to define a successful business strategy are correctly paired with the notion of what would prompt a disruption to the business plan execution and to achieving the business plan goals. Understanding what represents failure in a business plan and business strategy is essential and relevant to prevent the failure of the original business plan and business strategy. Indeed, the only action worse than a military defeat or failed business strategy is when you "reinforce defeat" and commit people, resources, and time to try to save a strategy or business venture that is already lost.

Commercial Exit Strategy Process Steps:

Step 1: Determine measures of effectiveness to establish performance of business plan.

Step 2: Create a "watch list" of customer, competition, and industry trends that could derail the business plan and strategy.

Step 3: Create three scenarios of possible events that would have low, medium, and high severity for the success of the business plan.

Step 4: Identify solutions to mitigate effects on company external and internal areas that will ensure success.

Step 5: Identify conditions for each scenario that would trigger a strategic exit and how to implement it.

Exit strategies and exit conditions are best thought of before a business plan or strategy is created and implemented. In that way, a business can successfully monitor both the positive and negative success measures for the business plan implementation to ensure that the plan is a success. Figure 15.1 is a worksheet that can serve as a valuable tool in creating an exit strategy.

Step 1: Determine Measures of Effectiveness to Establish Business Plan Performance

The role of the measures of effectiveness, both positive and negative, is to select two to three indicators that reflect the current state of the business plan and determine whether the plan is working. The success and failure indicators should be easy to understand, have a reliable data measurement and data storage process, and have a strong correlation to the business plan's success or failure, respectively. An example of indicators for a new product sales campaign would be the market share of the new product vs. the competition, tracking the opinions (positive and negative) of the new product, and looking at the price differential of the product vs. its competitors in major markets. These indicators, like a weather forecast, give you a strong general idea how the business plan and strategy are proceeding. Indicators rarely offer a 100% precise perspective on a plan's success or failure. Rather, the proper use of indicators to measure a strategy seek to balance quality indicators with available data against precise but hard to define indicators that may not have the data or measurement systems available.

The final test for indicator selection for a business team is to conduct a "common-sense" test to ensure that the indicators used reflect the true performance of the business. The final caution is to ensure that the business team can easily and accurately get the data necessary to measure the indicators. If the indicator data sources are spotty, infrequent, or subject to interpretation, the business team needs to select another data source or find a new indicator. Nothing ruins a measurement and strategy assessment process faster than bad data. All decisions made from bad data are suspect and soon thrown out.

Exit Strategy Step 1: Determine business strategy measures of effectiveness to track performance and non-performance of business plan.

	Time Period 1	Time Period 2	Time Period 3	Time Period 4	Time Period 5	Time Period 6	Time Period 7	Time Period 8	Time Period 9	Time Period 10	Time Period 11	Time Period 12
Positive Performance Metric 1												
Positive Performance Metric 2												
Positive Performance Metric 3												
Negative Non-Performance Metric 1												
Negative Non-Performance Metric 2												
Negative Non-Performance Metric 3												

Exit Strategy Step 2: Create a "Watch List" of Customer, Competition, and Industry Trends that Could Derail the Business Plan and Strategy.

	Time Period 1	Time Period 2	Time Period 3	Time Period 4	Time Period 5	Time Period 6	Time Period 7	Time Period 8	Time Period 9	Time Period 10	Time Period 11	Time Period 12
Customer Positive Perform Metric 1												
Competition Positive Perform Metric 2												
Industry Positive Perform Metric 3												
Customer Negative Perform Metric 1												
Competition Negative Perform Metric 2												
Industry Negative Perform Metric 3												

Exit Strategy Step 3:
Create Three Scenarios Of Possible Events That Would Be Low Strength, Medium Strength, And High Strength For The Success Of The Business Plan.

Business Strategy Scenario	Solution to Scenario #1 Low Strength Effect to Strategy	Solution to Scenario #2 Medium Strength Effect to Strategy	Solution to Scenario #3 High Strength Effect to Strategy
Company External Conditions			
Customer Conditions for Scenario			
Competition Conditions for Scenario			
Industry Conditions for Scenario			
Regulatory Conditions for Scenario			
Company Internal Conditions			
Cost Conditions for Scenario			
Labor Conditions for Scenario			
Legal Conditions for Scenario			
Profitability Conditions for Scenario			
Other Internal Conditions for Scenario			

Exit Strategy Step 4: Identify Solutions To Mitigate Effects On Company External and Internal Areas That Will Improve Performance.

Business Strategy Scenario	Solution to Scenario #1 Low Strength Effect to Strategy	Solution to Scenario #2 Medium Strength Effect to Strategy	Solution to Scenario #3 High Strength Effect to Strategy
Company Solution Steps to Influence			
Customer Conditions			
Competition Conditions			
Industry Conditions			
Regulatory Conditions			
Company Internal Action Steps			
Cost Conditions			
Labor Conditions			
Marketing Conditions			
Profitability Conditions			
Other Internal Conditions			

Exit Strategy Step 5 – Identify Conditions For Each Scenario That Would Trigger A Strategic Exit And How To Implement.

Business Strategy Scenario	Solution to Scenario #1 Low Strength Effect to Strategy	Solution to Scenario #2 Medium Strength Effect to Strategy	Solution to Scenario #3 High Strength Effect to Strategy
Negative Non-Performance Metric 1			
Negative Non-Performance Metric 2			
Negative Non-Performance Metric 3			
Company Internal Exit Action Steps			
Human Resources Exit Steps			
Marketing Exit Steps			
Finance Exit Steps			
Sales Force Exit Steps			
Public Relations Exit Steps			
Operating Exit Steps			

Figure 15.1 Commercial Exit Strategy Worksheet.

There should also be both positive measures of effectiveness, indicators, or data points—that show the plan is working—and negative measures of effectiveness, indicators, or data points—that show the plan is not working. The use of a measurement system for both positive and negative performance measures helps ensure that a business team is keeping a close eye on trends that show success or lack of success. Too often, business teams can become enthralled or personally tied to the success of a business plan; they have become so engaged in its success because of long hours, hard work, and a desire to be successful. The use in assessment and decision-making of both positive and negative measures of effectiveness is vital to ensure that the business team has a clear and unfettered picture of its standing and progress in the execution of its business strategy.

Step 2: Create a Watch List of Customer, Competition, and Industry Trends That Could Derail the Business Plan and Strategy

The creation of a watch list provides the business team with business trends, customers, and locations to track how major business environmental factors are affecting the progress of the business. U.S. Military Intelligence and threat analysts use the terms *target area of interest* (TAI) and *named area of interest* (NAI) to track the key elements and location of enemy combat power, TAIs, and key expected geographic locations to support the enemy's plan, NAIs. The concept is that the enemy will reveal its strategy as it moves through the landscape (force size and location) and according to what types of equipment (destructive power and capability) it decides to use.

The major business environmental factors that the corporation needs to concern itself with focus on customers, the competition, and other industry trends. The data gathered from these trends are rarely completely quantitative but contain rich qualitative insight into the likes, dislikes, and expected behavior of customers, competitors, and industry trends. Customers, competition, and industry trends are the primary factors that derail an effective business strategy.

Customer trends for a watch list concern major customer activities in the marketplace, changes in customer preferences or purchase behavior, changes in customer purchase priority or quantity, social trends driving purchase behavior, and new technology and capabilities that may create the demand for a new product or new features. An example of a customer trend that a company got partially correct was the launch of the Apple Newton in mid-1992. The Apple Newton was an innovative and dynamic personal digital assistant (PDA) that was Apple's first move into the personal digital devices that have brought Apple so much renown and success. Despite Apple's innovation, the Newton was expensive, slow, and prone to fail to recognize handwriting. Apple got the customer trend right, but the technology was not there yet.

The competition is equally as important to track as customer trends. Competitive trends to watch include: new product and service announcements from the company Web site; customer testimonials and product reviews, appearing in leading national and industry media publications; changes in how competitive products and services are packaged, priced, and displayed for purchase; the introduction of new and leading-edge technologies; and any major financial changes (positive and negative) for the competition. The competition needs to include both direct and indirect competitors so the firm is fully aware of all the trends of the competitive forces arrayed against it. For a fast-food restaurant, the direct competition would include other fast-food restaurants; the indirect competition would be price discounts or lower priced menu items of sit-down restaurant chains, as well as grocery and other stores that offer a pre-cooked food pickup service. All of these competitors offer both a direct and indirect challenge to the fast-food restaurant's customer base.

The final trend area to observe are changes and transitions occurring within the industry in which the corporation competes. Industry trends include changes in the legal and regulatory landscape that affect how the corporation makes and sells its products; changes in the economy, employment, or regional landscapes that affect how the customer base or corporation makes, distributes, and sells the product; and major societal trends that affect how the corporation makes, distributes, and sells its products. A recent example of how changes in industry trends have vastly affected an industry is clearly shown in the housing industry. Beginning in 2008, new home sales started to decline, as the U.S. economy sank into a severe recession. Coupled with slowing demand was the blowup in the U.S. mortgage security market, which dried up the available financial pool of available capital for mortgages. The U.S. housing industry, still producing an in-demand product of good quality, was delivered a double whammy—both by lowered demand and by an almost complete dry-up of capital to fund new mortgages. Again, as in both the examples of customer trends and competitive trends, the business team has to seek quantitative and qualitative data to identify the most significant trends for the watch list.

Step 3: Create Three Scenarios of Possible Events That Would Have Low, Medium, and High Severity for the Success of the Business Plan

The next step in the creation of an exit strategy is for the business team to create three business scenarios that would influence the successful conclusion of the business in terms of low, medium, and high severity. The creation of three scenarios is not meant to encompass the full range of possibilities that the firm could expect to influence the successful conclusion of its business plan. Rather, the use of three scenarios of low, medium, and high severity has the expected effects assigned to company external conditions and company internal conditions. The end state of this step is having three likely scenarios that affect the successful conclusion of the business plan in low, medium, and high severity with the estimated company external and company internal effects identified.

The first part of step 3 is to take the most likely customer, competitor, industry, and regulatory trends identified in step 2 and to create low, medium, and high severity events across the three scenarios. An example of a scenario impact would be the competitor lowering prices by 5%, 10%, and 20% for the low, medium, and high severity scenarios, respectively. These customer, competitor, and industry trends can be quantitative but, most likely, are qualitative observations on the conditions of customer, competitor, industry, and regulatory conditions that affect the successful implementation of the business plan. The area of regulatory conditions has been added to steps 3 through 5 for scenario planning to address any possible changes in local, state, federal, or other applicable laws and governing regulations. The area of company internal conditions is present to plan for any ideas such as budget reductions, production cost increases, or higher profitability goals that would affect the successful business plan execution.

The business team can decide to use as many factors as possible in scenario planning, or the team may only change a few to create the scenarios. For example, the low, medium, and high scenarios may have only a competitor price decrease action and a company production cost increase to challenge the business team with pricing decisions and cost saving measures in order to be able to meet the original financial goals. The items on the worksheet represent only a few of the possibilities to change. As a note of caution, the business team may want to use only two to four variables when creating each scenario. The overuse of variables can lead to an overly complex and unwieldy mitigation plan in step 4.

Step 4: Identify Solutions to Mitigate Effects on Company External and Internal Areas That Ensure Success

The goal of step 4 is for the team to develop actions that mitigate the effects of the negative items identified in step 3. The business team should create specific mitigation actions and planning steps for both company external conditions and company internal conditions that the business team can implement or plan to implement to help ensure that the plan is a success. For example, if the business team identified a competitor price reduction as a threat, the business team will want to identify specific actions to mitigate the effects of the competitor's price cuts. For example, the business team may identify a 60-day advertising campaign comparing the improved attributes of the company product vs. the competition, a 30-day use of discount coupons for repeat customers, and a 2-week period when the business honors the competitor's price for a closely related item as the action steps to mitigate the competition in one of these scenarios.

For each of the three scenarios, low, medium, and high, the business team should brainstorm to develop plans and activities that can mitigate the effects of customer, competitor, and industry conditions so the plan can succeed. The team needs to be creative in its solutions; innovative in application and design; and very precise in how to plan, resource, and implement each of the identified action steps. If the team identifies a highly likely effect from the customer, competitor, industry, or regulatory, the business team should immediately add the mitigation steps and plan to the existing business plan.

Good ideas to mitigate negative effects on the success of the business plan should be added if they could serve to prevent a bad action. For example, if the business team hears rumors of a new competitor advertising campaign, it may automatically construct its own advertising campaign to mitigate the effectiveness of the competition. Other mitigation plans, such as price cuts or additional expenses, may be left in a planning stage until there is cause to implement them. The business team must weigh the benefit of a preventive use of a mitigation action (i.e., a price cut) vs. the benefits of retaining the mitigation item (i.e., the revenue value of the price cut) and only using it when required. Step 4 is vitally important because a business team can use creativity and insight to have pre-built reaction plans to the most likely negative scenarios that could damage the success of the business plan. Pre-built plans help guarantee success and help identify weaknesses or vulnerabilities with the business plan early so their potentially catastrophic consequences can be avoided.

Step 5: Identify Conditions for Each Scenario That Trigger a Strategic Exit and How to Implement It

The final step in the creation of an exit strategy is to identify what are the final conditions or metrics that trigger the execution of the business exit plan. After all of the mitigation efforts created in step 4 have been implemented and have not been successful, the business requires a line in the sand to define an end, when the business plan will be discontinued and the exit from the business initiated. This is important because, unless there is a definable set of measures to signal when an exit occurs, the business could continue indefinitely to fund and support the failingly business venture with no end in sight. Businesses that do not end funding to failingly ventures waste valuable resources and people's time, and they damage morale. Most importantly, by the continued funding of failing ventures, businesses deny potential funding to other successful ventures that could use the resources to expand.

The first part of step 5 is to identity what the final trigger or line in the sand is on the negative business performance metrics that cause a firm to initiate an exit strategy. This can be three or more non-performance metrics, it could be a single value, or it could be the value after one month to a year. The market share percentage is an important measure when looking at how much share of a market a company has. A company may state that if its market share falls below 10%, after the company has implemented its mitigation steps, that it has failed, and it will exit the market. These decisions are unique to each company. The most important point is for a company to decide and agree what constitutes the non-performance metric and the metrics value to trigger an exit.

The final part of step 5 is to create an action plan to execute the exit strategy. For example, if this were the closing of a retail store that was not successful, the closing would trigger a number of company actions. Human Resources would have to find new positions at different stores for employees, Finance would decide whether a discounted sale or movement of inventory to other stores made sense, Real Estate would look at breaking the store lease or subleasing, etc. This would not be an exhaustive list, but it would seek to identify the major steps to be taken to execute the exit strategy. This execution is vital because the faster the company executes the exit strategy, the more money it saves, and the faster resources can be redirected to other more successful areas.

Exit Strategy Personal Step: Ensure You Have a Well-Described Exit Strategy for Your Career

Just as military strategies and business plans have exit strategies, civilian careers need to consider exit strategies to ensure that your personal career plans and aspirations remain on track. Personal career management needs to monitor trends with customers, competitors, and the industry to ensure that you remain in the best possible corporation, industry, and career track. At times, you may have to consider a lateral shift, demotion, or a change of employer to continue to learn, gain new experience, and gain additional responsibilities in order to meet your career goals. Another area of growing importance is the lifestyle associated with the new career field under consideration. The use of the watch list items in step 2 is extraordinarily helpful for you to ensure that you are in the correct customer base, company division, and industry that will allow you to move forward in your career. At times, certain industries and companies may slow, but there will always be bosses and business segments that are "hot" for the company's future success.

If you decide that you need to leave a company or industry, you need to do a detailed transition plan complete with Primary-Alternate-Contingency-Emergency (P-A-C-E) back-up plans, as discussed in Chapter 12, to ensure that you have a successful and uneventful career transition. For any career transition, the creation and analysis of a watch list for new opportunities, companies, and industries can be especially helpful to ensure that you move into a "hot" or stable area and not into an area that is threatened by customer loss, strong competition, or a declining industry.

Summary

The methodology presented in this chapter is a detailed and semi-quantitative approach to help a business identify points of vulnerability in a business plan, plan to mitigate those effects, and the plan to exit the business if necessary. You can carry out this process with a high degree of success by getting a varied and experienced group of business professionals around a table and running through this process. Even if the business team spends two hours identifying how it will define and track success and failure, trends to watch that could derail its business plan, how various trends would cause a scenario to challenge the business, solutions to mitigate the negative effects of trends, and the final decision points when a business plan has been deemed a failure and what steps to take, the business will have a tremendous advantage because of the team's efforts.

The key point of difference is that the majority of business people expect a business plan to succeed and, all too often, ignore the signs of failure in the market or with the competition. Based on your combat and non-combat mission experience, you expect a military plan to be instantly challenged and changed as a result of changes in the environment, the enemy, and available resources. Therefore, you must have multiple actions planned to rescue the original plan so the business plan can be successful. The bottom line is that all plans are challenged, no matter how good the planning and coordination efforts. The central additional task in determining how well a company plans its original business plan is that it must also plan just as well to mitigate the possible primary negative effects of the market and competition and ensure that the business plan is a success.

On a personal career note, as veterans, you need to have clear, defined, and open career expectations so you know how to exit your current position, career field, company, or industry if events align to derail your career plans. You want your career aspirations and career goals to remain heading in the right direction. Business leaders, organizational structures, companies, and industries change and transform at an alarming rate. The possession of personal career exit strategies and personal career watch lists of vital market trends will ensure that your career remains on track and a success.

Note

1. Stewart, Richard W. "Staff Operations: The X Corps in Korea, December 1950," The Combat Studies Institute, Fort Leavenworth, Kansas, April 1991.

Section 4

Improve

Improve

The ability not only to lead an organization but also to improve an organization is one of the hallmarks of a great leader. Improvement is more than identifying weaknesses in people and processes. True improvement is marked by sustained improvement, coupled with the ability to get organizations to change dynamically on their own, and for individuals to be able to identify confidently, successfully, and productively the change they need to make in their career or job performance to attain their career goals. Finally, personal, organizational, and employee improvement is not a one-time event. Great improvement is continuous, employs action plans, scheduled learning, and follow-up plans to ensure that the improvement happens and remains in the organization. You need to not only help your company succeed but help other veterans succeed. Use the after-action review to focus on improving key operations, the counseling session to improve employee performance, and other military processes to help fill other commercial needs.

CHAPTER 16

VETERAN LESSON 16: USE THE MILITARY AFTER-ACTION REVIEW

The military after-action review (AAR) is a fantastic process to dissect a complex operation to determine what happened, what went right, what needs to be done better, and what steps need to be taken to ensure the operation improves the next time. The military spends a great deal of time, energy, manpower, training, and resources to ensure that all personnel, from the Navy to the Air Force, are properly trained to accomplish their mission successfully in combat.

The Military Perspective on the AAR

The AAR is a dominant force in military culture, and its use has been adopted into all training and operations, ranging from a company live-fire training event to daily combat operations to even how mundane supplies are purchased. On a daily basis, across the globe, and in operational environments ranging from combat patrols to dining facility operations to aircraft carrier landings, there are hundreds of AARs in progress. Furthermore, all ranks in the military conduct AARs, from admirals to captains to airman. All of these AARs have one goal in mind: how to perform operations more effectively in terms of people, time, and resources and how to produce a mission outcome of higher quality. On the battlefield, a good AAR saves lives of both soldiers and civilians. In the commercial business world, a good AAR can create new customers, cut costs, and help create innovative new product revenue for the company.

The Commercial AAR Has Unsurpassed Business Potential

If the military completely embraces the concept of the AAR, the commercial business world has some understanding of how to apply the AAR concept to its planning, employee career development, and operations. The commercial world does not have a defined nonquantitative process to determine how to perform a systematic and constructive review of a process, business plan, or operation and make that process better. Existing quantitative process improvement protocols, such as Six Sigma, Lean, and Lean Six Sigma to name only a few, are fairly narrowly scoped processes that provide the quantitative tools and statistical knowledge to improve a process, but they often do not provide a strategic perspective of a business process or plan.

The nonquantitative review of a business plan or process is vital, because the employee acceptance and underlying value placed in these processes usually drive the quantitative portion of the business process. The most essential part of the military AAR process to be translated is the ability to create, to nurture, and to sustain an atmosphere that allows for the examination of existing operations, mistakes, and areas of improvement that encourages and supports improvement. You may initially struggle with creating a culture of trust so employees feel free to identify and correct areas of business deficiency. Your challenge is to avoid making the commercial AAR a witch hunt. Rather, the commercial AAR process strives to be a platform to launch the business into the next higher level, for improved operational and financial results. The commercial AAR process is a critical component that encourages and allows employees to understand what they did, what went right, what could be better, and how to make it better.

Preparing for the Commercial AAR

There are a few administrative steps to ensure that the AAR is a productive and efficient use of time. First, the AAR needs a quiet, dedicated room for the entire session. The room needs to have whiteboards, a video screen, Internet access, and a supply of writing devices, to ensure that findings and action items are recorded. Additionally, the use of video for recording discussions and action items can be especially useful for ensuring that everyone has the same record for the AAR and its result. The use of a private room with resources maintains the focus on the AAR and prevents disruptions. Second, cellphones and PDAs should be kept in a box or another location in the room, to ensure every employee's focus on the AAR as it is ongoing. Cellphones can be redistributed for breaks or as required.

Third, the AAR needs to use a controlled and agreed-upon timeline so that all areas of the AAR are accomplished. This also helps keep the focus, attention, and motivation of the group so that an AAR does not "bog down" in unimportant discussion but remains focused on all the steps. Fourth, the day of the week for the AAR should be a Tuesday to Thursday, to leave Monday and Friday for work items. Fifth, the AAR should have some type of refreshments and scheduled breaks so all employees are comfortable and attentive. Setting the room up in a "U" or similar shape where everyone can see the other faces of the people involved helps contribute to an open environment—so people look at faces and not the back of people's heads. Finally, the person(s) leading the commercial AAR should encourage and promote an open and encouraging environment to ensure a focus on understanding and improving the business operation. The use of humorous and creative YouTube videos, upbeat music, and the like can help keep the room atmosphere light, focused, and attentive.

Commercial AAR Steps

There are four key steps to the commercial AAR (see Figure 16.1):

Step 1: Establish an environment for review and introspection.
Step 2: Provide a brief overview of what happened and divide the operation into segments.
Step 3: Identify strengths, weaknesses, and recommendations for improvement in each business function.
Step 4; Create an action plan for improvement, and follow-up to ensure that the improvements are happening.

Step 1: Establish an Environment for Review and Introspection

Establishing and fostering an environment and a culture of improvement is, by far, the most difficult and the most important for a relevant and productive AAR process. An environment of improvement is, by its very nature, an open and questioning environment that rests upon a goal of being the best. There is a significant difference between an organization saying, "We want to be the best," and an organization to acting as though, "We want to be the best." The very nature of improvement is challenging and difficult.

Atmospheres of improvement help build excellence. I was conducting some training for General Electric (GE) at its famed Crotonville leadership training center in upstate New York along the Hudson River. I was paired with some new GE employees, and we set off conducting a business case analysis to develop a new product marketing plan for one of the various GE businesses. The goal for this project, after two long days of work, was to present the business case analysis and business plan to three senior GE executives. We were half way through our analysis when our smooth presentation came to a grinding halt under a barrage of questions surrounding customer preferences, cash flow, advertising strategies, and competitive analysis. The message that executives were sending was clear: business plans need to be overwhelmingly detailed and finely executed to achieve the business results. This business analysis helped build the vital importance of maintaining an open atmosphere for improvement.

Step 2: Provide a Brief Overview of What Happened and Divide the Operation into Segments

The next step in the AAR process is to get all parties to agree on what happened, when it happened, and who did (or did not) do it. The simple step of achieving a general group agreement of what happened and when can entirely derail an AAR process. The AAR process can easily become confused when the major actors disagree on what did or did not happen, who were the actors involved, and what was the result or lack of result of their actions. The bottom line is that

Step 1: Prepare the Environment for a Commercial After Action Review

Business Event _____   Dates Covered _____

Employees Attending
1. _____   6. _____
2. _____   7. _____
3. _____   8. _____
4. _____   9. _____
5. _____   10. _____

Business Mission Statement and Plan of Action:

Step 2: Describe What Happened and Divide the Operation into Segments

Business Actor	Time Period +1	Time Period +2	Time Period +3	Time Period +4	Time Period +5	Time Period +6
Business Plan Segment						
Actor A						
Actor B						
Actor C						
Actor D						
Actor E						
Actor F						

Step 3: Identify Strengths, Weaknesses, and Recommendations for Improvement for Each Segment

	Time Period +1	Time Period +2	Time Period +3	Time Period +4	Time Period +5	Time Period +6
Business Plan Segment						
What Went Well						
What Went Well						
What Went Well						
What Needs Improvement						
What Needs Improvement						
What Needs Improvement						
Ideas to Improve						
Ideas to Improve						
Ideas to Improve						

Step 4: Create an Action Plan for Improvement

	Weaknesses 1	Weaknesses 2	Weaknesses 3	Weaknesses 4	Weaknesses 5	Weaknesses 6
Weakness Name						
2nd Round Vote Score						
Identification of the item / task / product to be improved						
Description of how improving this item will improve the business execution						
Specific listing defining and describing the problem						
Measurement system and plan to measure existing and future changes						
Listing of all employees involved in the improvement process						
Specific action items, dates for training, re-training, or product improvement that will improve the business function						
Dates and plan to re-assess the improved business function to ensure the improvement was successful						

Other Remarks and Follow-Up Items:
1. _____
2. _____
3. _____

Figure 16.1 Commercial After-Action Review Worksheet.

the AAR timeline does not have to be 100% correct, but all participants in the AAR have to agree that the timeline, actors involved, the actions, and the results are generally correct. Several tools can be very helpful to sort through this process. Again, this is a process to establish what happened. It is not a process to establish who failed, what did not occur, or what should have happened. The goal is to reach agreement on the events involved in the business plan or business process so the business team can examine the actions and results to achieve improvement.

A number of simple tools can make Step 2 much easier. The first action is to appoint two people as a primary and secondary recorders. The first person records the actions and results in the timeline, and the second recorder takes notes of employee's remarks. The use of two recorders with a running written record of AAR comments is especially helpful for a written record. In addition, the use of a video recorder can speed this action step along. The second action is the use of a timeline. A time-event timeline is one of the more helpful tools to use during the AAR process to analyze what happened and to determine which person or business actor did what. The timeline can be simple to arrange in days or hours along the X or horizontal axis and the actors involved along the Y or vertical axis. The boxes that are created in the intersection of the time period and the actor are the actions with the subsequent results. A team using the process of a recorder and a timeline can work through a disagreement as it occurs. Finally, once the timeline is complete, the employee AAR team members can divide the business operation into major segments (i.e., planning, preparation, execution, etc.) if that helps them understand what happened and why. If the employee AAR team has reached general agreement on the timeline, who did what, and what was the result of their actions, the AAR timeline is complete. The employee team must pay close attention to the established schedule for the AAR so it does not use too much time determining what happened vs. improving business operations and the subsequent results.

Step 3: Identify Strengths, Weaknesses, and Recommendations for Improvement in Each Business Function

Once the employee team has determined what happened, it needs to determine what went well, what did not go well, and how to improve the process. The danger in this part of the AAR is becoming sidelined onto one or two items and not fully assessing the areas that require improvement and how to improve them. Following the initial AAR schedule, established as part of the administrative segment of setting up the AAR, it is critical to allow sufficient time to identify strength, weakness, and recommendations for improvement.

The identification of strengths is to ensure that the employee team knows what it does well and understands that those items are critical to the continued success of the company. The weaknesses are important because they form the core area for the improvement action plan in Step 4. As the team goes through the entire timeline to identify the critical weaknesses that need to be improved, it should create a running list of all the weaknesses that could be part of the improvement action plan.

The employee team should use a multi-round, weighted voting process to determine the top three or four items to work on for the action plan. To perform weighted voting, each team member is given five yellow sticky notes with his or her name on them. Each of the weakness items is written onto a white sheet of 8½ × 11" paper and spread onto the walls or whiteboards around the room. To vote, each team member distributes the sticky notes on the associated 8½ × 11" sheet of paper. Each team member is allowed up to three votes maximum per weakness, with no more than five total votes per person. At the end of the first round of voting, the vote results are tallied, and the sticky notes given back to each team member. The weaknesses are rank ordered, in descending order of votes (the highest first), and the list is divided in half so that only the highest voted items remain. The second round of voting occurs in the same manner, and the weaknesses are again listed in descending order. The top three or four items after the second round of voting are the weakness to be addressed in the action plan.

The final step after the top weaknesses are identified is for the employee team to work each item for recommendations how to improve each weakness. The team should identify specific, concrete, and identifiable action items that will help improve the performance of the weakness area. The multiround, weighted voting process can be used if there is disagreement or a lack of consensus on how to select the specific action items to improve the weaknesses.

Step 4: Create an Action Plan for Improvement, and Follow Up to Ensure That the Improvements Are Happening

Anyone who has led a handful of AARs knows the excitement of the AAR, getting the entire team motivated to improve, and identifying items that need to be improved. However, the same AAR leaders can be dismayed later when the same problems happen repeatedly. The problem is that there is no AAR action plan with scheduled follow-ups to correct the errors. The creation of an AAR action plan for improvement is the most important part of the AAR process. It is relatively easy to identify what did not go well and what needs to be done to improve the process. The entire point of an AAR is to improve operations definitely, and the action plan is the critical element of the improvement process.

The action plan is relatively simple to complete. The most difficult part of the action plan is to get the resources and time from all participants to ensure that the improvements happen.

The action plan needs to have the following to be complete:

(1) Identification of the item, task, or product to be improved.
(2) Description of how improving this item will improve the business execution.
(3) Specific listing defining and describing the problem.
(4) Measurement system and definition of how to measure the current state and measure subsequent improvement in the process.
(5) Listing of all employees involved in the improvement process.
(6) Specific action items and dates for training, retraining, or product improvement sessions that will improve the business function.

(7) Dates and plan to reassess the improved business function to ensure that the improvement was successful.

The action plan is critical so that there are universal expectations on what needs to be done and when to improve the business function. Additionally, there needs to be a measurement process and retesting aspect of the improvement plan to ensure that the improvement goals identified in the AAR are achieved. Finally, the action plan is not only composed of items that were identified as weaknesses in the AAR. The employee team may have to schedule sessions to maintain and expand its strengths in order to maintain those strengths as a competitive advantage of its business.

Summary

One of the key mistakes that is made in the AAR process is an immediate transition into what went wrong, who was to blame, and how the organization cannot allow that to happen again. Good AARs seek to understand what occurred, what went well, what did not go well. After the entire group understands and agrees about what happened, the AAR team formulates a plan, timeline, and responsibility to ensure that the right actions continue and that the deficient items are corrected and improved. Any focus on blame, denying responsibility, overdominance by the leader in AAR topic discussions, ignoring critical issues, an abandonment of critical thought to identify the improvement areas, or a solid follow-up plan to improve the deficient areas will render all of the activities in the AAR process valueless to improve the organization. AARs demand honesty, hard work, a team approach, and an overall commitment to improvement.

The AAR process needs to be well organized, respect everyone's time and opinion, and build a culture of openness and improvement so the entire team constantly and consistently seeks to improve its operations. Finally, a great AAR creates an improvement plan with assigned responsibilities and an implementation timeline to ensure that the improvements are done. Great AARs not only identify improvement areas, they create plans to improve and ensure that the improvement happens.

CHAPTER 17

VETERAN LESSON 17: EMPLOY COUNSELING SESSIONS

In most commercial businesses, there are two or three mandatory performance review sessions where employees and their immediate supervisors conduct the semi-annual and annual performance reviews. The quality of these sessions varies tremendously, as does the quality of the career progression advice. The overall goal of the corporate performance review is to improve employee performance and to offer ideas about how employees can improve their opportunities for promotion. Ideally, the business performance review provides employees with definitive examples of how they performed well during the year, what they need to improve, steps they can take to improve their results, and the next steps they can take to reach their career goals.

However, in numerous instances, the supervisors of employees struggle to deliver this simple yet highly valuable career guidance to employees. On the other side of the employee performance review, the vast majority of employees want more direct, simple, and actionable performance items that they can use to make themselves into better employees. Employees want to be higher performers, and supervisors want to deliver more concrete and actionable performance items. Your knowledge of the military performance counseling session translated to business is a way for you to distinguish yourself in the corporation.

Military Personnel Performance Improves through Performance Counseling

You recognize that the military counseling session is an excellent tool to improve the performance of military personnel, and it can be directly applied to improve the performance of commercial business employees. The military uses the performance counseling session in monthly, quarterly, or as-required sessions to list the standards of performance, how the soldier is doing to meet the performance standard, and what the soldier must do in the future to improve or surpass performance standard.

The military counseling session is a simple and complete document that is defined as follows. The military counseling statement contains: (1) a description of the standard of performance at which the position or task must be performed, (2) a description of the military member's performance in comparison to the standard of performance, and (3) a description stating the precise steps the soldier must take in order for his or her performance to meet the standard. The military performance counseling sessions also provide written performance records that can be used in follow-up sessions to ensure that the soldier is improving. Most importantly, the written performance record provides a valuable guide to enable the soldier to understand how to improve his or her performance. Indeed, a performance counseling session may appear to some soldiers as only a record of negative performance, but all soldiers know that personal, leader-to-subordinate counseling is an exceptionally valuable tool for subordinates to improve and surpass their career goals. The high level of personal career attention to employee improvement and subordinate development is an incredibly valuable tool for the development of business professionals.

The Purpose of Employee Performance Counseling

The first step to construct an employee performance counseling session in a workplace is to ensure that all parties understand that these sessions are designed to improve performance. The performance counseling session should be planned two to four weeks in advance, to allow both you and the employee adequate time to prepare and clear your schedules. In addition, the subject and time covered in the performance counseling session should be established two to four weeks in advance and be clear to you both. For example, "Jessica, in 30 days, I would like to discuss with you your performance in your major duties during the second quarter of 2010. During the meeting, please bring your business results, ideas for how I can help you improve your performance, and how we can help prepare you for your next promotion."

The performance counseling session should also be in a neutral setting, such as a common conference room, that is in a quiet, removed location and away from any distractions. Additionally, the supervisor should set a day of the week, ideally not a Monday or another day that is a heavier than normal workload for the employee, that will allow the employee to prepare and concentrate fully. The use of these preparations for the employee performance counseling session ensures that the employee is prepared, understands the purpose for the counseling session, and has a time and spatial setting that encourages him or her to focus on work performance and career goals.

Employee Performance Counseling Steps

Step 1: Set the counseling stage.
Step 2: Describe the employee's performance and the company's accepted standards of performance.

Step 3: Evaluate the employee's performance and create an action plan to improve.

Step 4: Make the counseling a success: follow up, motivate, assist, and keep on track.

These four steps outlined in Figure 17.1 ensure that there is a process during the performance counseling session that leads not only to the identification of areas of improvement but, more importantly, leads to how to improve and how that improvement will be measured.

Step 1: Set the Counseling Stage

The most important part of the performance counseling session takes place before you and the employee even meet. You must create and maintain a performance culture atmosphere that encourages productive performance reviews and the self-identification of areas of improvement in order to advance the employee's career. Once a time, agenda, and location have been established for the performance counseling session, begin pre-work to describe precisely the work performance of the employee.

Step 2: Describe the Employee's Performance and the Company's Accepted Standards of Performance

The critical element of describing the employee's performance and describing the company's accepted standards of performance are to be specific and detailed and to remove emotion from the performance counseling session. Any person who has every been in the military remembers quite well one of his or her first performance counseling sessions that began, "I don't like it when you . . ." My instance of an inadequate military performance counseling session happened in Ranger School during the Benning Phase, when one of the ranger instructors pulled me aside and said, "I don't like how you crossed that linear danger zone; you need to do it better." My reaction was instant shut down, and I began to ignore those things that the ranger instructor had said, even though he was probably correct.

In performance counseling sessions, when you let emotion take over and the session moves away from specific standards, both you and the employee have lost your objective for the performance counseling session. The supervisor has lost the opportunity to improve the employee's performance, and the employee has lost the opportunity to improve. Ultimately, the company is the largest loser in this inter-action, because the overall standards will not improve. When precise facts and standards are used, the mood of the session turns toward improvement.

The first step is to establish the facts and rationale behind the employee's actions for both good behavior and the behavior that needs to be improved. The supervisor needs to be very specific in the who, what, when, where, and why (back to the military mission statement format) of the employee's performance. For example, a supervisor is discussing a call at an inbound customer call center, "John, I noticed on Wednesday at the 59th Street Call Center that you took four times the average

Commercial Counseling Session Worksheet

Job Title: _____

Employee Name: _____

Counselor Name: _____

Session Date: _____

Period Covered: _____

Evaluated Items	Base or Goal	Qtr 1	Qtr 2	Qtr 3	Qtr 4	Full Year
Item 1	Numeric Qty	Numeric Qty	Numeric Qty	Numeric Qty	Numeric Qty	Numeric Qty
Item 2	Numeric Qty	Numeric Qty	Numeric Qty	Numeric Qty	Numeric Qty	Numeric Qty
Item 3	Numeric Qty	Numeric Qty	Numeric Qty	Numeric Qty	Numeric Qty	Numeric Qty
Item 4	Numeric Qty	Numeric Qty	Numeric Qty	Numeric Qty	Numeric Qty	Numeric Qty

Performance vs. Goal	Met Goal?	Qtr 1	Qtr 2	Qtr 3	Qtr 4	Full Year
Item 1	Yes or No?	+/- % Ch from goal	+/- % Ch from goal	+/- % Ch from goal	+/- % Ch from goal	+/- % Ch from goal
Item 2	Yes or No?	+/- % Ch from goal	+/- % Ch from goal	+/- % Ch from goal	+/- % Ch from goal	+/- % Ch from goal
Item 3	Yes or No?	+/- % Ch from goal	+/- % Ch from goal	+/- % Ch from goal	+/- % Ch from goal	+/- % Ch from goal
Item 4	Yes or No?	+/- % Ch from goal	+/- % Ch from goal	+/- % Ch from goal	+/- % Ch from goal	+/- % Ch from goal

Summary of Performance Including Evaluated Items:

1. _____
2. _____
3. _____

Summary of Items / Tasks Requiring Improvement:

1. _____
2. _____
3. _____

Summary of Personal Improvement Plan:

1. _____
2. _____
3. _____

Employee Professional Development and Career Advancement Steps:

1. _____
2. _____
3. _____

Figure 17.1 Commercial Counseling Session Worksheet.

time to answer a customer's question. This caused some additional calls to be routed to your fellow team members and delayed their lunch hour by 30 minutes. Ultimately, you answered the customer's question, and she rated her call experience an 8 out of 10, which is excellent. Can you explain what took so long to answer on the call?"

This is a critical step in the execution of the performance counseling session. First, the facts surrounding the employee's performance were established. Next, the supervisor asked the employee what specifically occurred to determine the rationale for the behavior. In the performance counseling session, it is essential that you clearly establish what happened but then also ensure that you support the employee in the decision. Then you work to discover why employees did what they did–in order to maintain employee morale and to continue to encourage employee initiative. The objective for the performance counseling session is for the supervisor to have employees who meet and exceed the company's standards, but also to have employees who exercise their initiative to solve unanticipated problems quickly.

Suppose that the employee responds, "The reason it took me so long to answer the call is that the customer originally called for a service issue, which was solved in about five minutes, within the average call time, but then the customer had both a billing problem and an address change. I remained on the call with the customer while accounting came on to solve the billing problem and perform the address change." This is a great performance counseling exchange. The supervisor states the performance observed, and the employee follows up with an explanation of the action. This allows for an even exchange and learning to take place.

The supervisor concludes this part of the performance counseling session as follows, "John, that was a great use of initiative to solve all of the customer's problems on the call, and it was reflected in the customer's evaluation of an 8 out of 10 in the after-call survey. We still need to ensure that we meet the 5-minute average call window, because that average time standard dictates how we do staffing, schedule breaks, and schedule training sessions. Next, let's move on and discuss some additional training and opportunities that we can do that will reinforce your good performance as well as make you better positioned for a promotion." This conversation reinforces the company standard, as well as reinforces the employee's good behavior, initiative, and problem solving, but sets the stage for moving to improve the employee's performance.

Step 3: Evaluate the Employee's Performance and Create an Action Plan to Improve

Your evaluation of the employee's performance must be precisely compared to the observed behavior and company behavior identified in Step 2. This format is to be used in order to reinforce job performance that the employee is doing well and to identify what the employee needs to improve and the company standard that the job performance needs to meet. Finally, the job performance that the employee needs to improve must have specific, understandable, and achievable action steps that the employee can take and achieve over the next 30 to 60 days to improve his or her performance.

The crucial part of Step 3 is for the supervisor to identify and explain clearly the variance in the employee's performance. The determination of the performance variance is a relatively simple process, as follows:

Employee Performance – Company Standard = + /− Performance Variance
  A Negative Performance Variance Value (−) Is When an Employee Is below the Company Standard
  A Positive Performance Variance Value (+) Is When an Employee Is above the Company Standard

This performance variance can be positive: if the employee exceeds the company standard, the performance variance is positive. If the employee performance variance is negative, the employee does not meet the company performance standard.

For those instances where the employee exceeds the company standard, the action items are to make the employee better in those areas and to identify special projects so that the employee can expand his or her leadership and skill sets. For example, if the company standard for a salesperson is to make five sales a week and the counseled employee has been making ten sales a week for the past six weeks, that employee's performance variance needs to direct his or her supervisor to a special project, new opportunity, or promotion possibility that can utilize those skills. When an employee has a positive performance variance, the supervisor should start to increase the level of responsibility to develop the employee's potential. Positive performance variance is a strong indicator for an employee who is ready for new challenges, responsibilities, and additional work projects. Furthermore, this employee should expand and build his or her leadership skill sets to improve the performance of other employees in the area where they perform well.

When there is a negative performance variance, the supervisor needs to help the employee identify the extent of the performance variance and identify action steps that the employee can take to reduce and reverse the performance variance. In order to perform Step 3 properly, there has to be good detail in the identification of the employee's performance and the company's standards undertaken in Step 2. If there is a good level of variance identified, it is much easier to create succinct action steps for employees to improve their level of performance. For example, using the example of an employee's level of sales again, if the employee is selling three units of product a week and the company standard is five, the employee needs to be put on an action plan to sell two more units a week.

Action steps have to lead directly to improved results. Simply telling an employee to "sell two more units a week" is not an action step. The example action steps to achieve two more sales a week to meet the company standard of five sales a week are as follows: (1) shadow salesperson X and salesperson Y for two days each to learn how they beat the standard, (2) work with marketing to develop a new advertising campaign to the salesperson's customer base, and (3) study the competition's products to reemphasize the value sell points for the sales call. The goal for the salesperson is to perform these three action steps over the next 30–60 days so he or she can raise sales from three a week to five a week in order to be in compliance with the company's weekly product goal. These are action steps that are specific, concrete, understandable, and can be completed by the employee to bring his or her level of performance in line with the company standard.

Step 4: Make the Counseling a Success: Follow Up, Motivate, Assist, and Keep on Track

Good follow-through and helping employees successfully complete their follow-up action steps is step 4 of the employee performance counseling process. The final action in performance counseling is for the supervisor to remember the employee, the action plan, or the items discussed, both good and bad, in the employee performance counseling session. The supervisor and the employee should set calendar reminders for the next two and four weeks to have another sit-down meeting to discuss the action steps, the employee's initial progress, and, if the action steps are working, for the employee to meet his or her performance goal. The use of dates, combined with specific action steps to meet a standard of performance that is understood by both parties, is a powerful motivator for both you and the employee.

You serve in the role of coach, cheer squad, and teacher—to keep the employee moving toward improving performance. The employee keeps an open line of communication to the supervisor and, through the action steps, uses self-initiative to improve performance to meet the goal. In the end, the success of performance counseling is evaluated by the ability of the employee to meet and exceed the business objectives. A final note is the use of performance measures, which are understood, accessible, and defined by both employee and supervisor. Such measures make it a black-and-white discussion of achieving or not achieving the company's performance standards.

Summary

Employee performance counseling sessions are a win-win-win event for the entire organization: you, the employee, and the corporation. You win because you have a productive, standards-based discussion with employees to improve their performance and prepare them for promotion and increased responsibility. Employees win because they have a precise situation identified of how they performed, had the correct standard of behavior identified, and then had an action plan created and supervised by their supervisor. Furthermore, the performance counseling session is an ideal setting for employees to observe, learn, and understand what they need to do to be better at their existing positions as well as prepare for promotion. The corporation wins because it has supervisors who are able to have productive sessions with employees to enable them to perform to a higher standard.

A supervisor and employee working together to raise performance standards is the gold standard for organizations to improve. This model of performance counseling, multiplied by hundreds and thousands of annual sessions, will create a better corporate organization and business performance. Finally and most importantly, performance counseling identifies and evaluates all behavior, not just bad. Good behavior has to be reinforced just as much or more than bad behavior. Employees need to know that their supervisors observe and appreciate their good actions.

Performance counseling sessions need to be performed as often as they are needed. Formal sessions can be monthly, but informal sessions can be daily, as the supervisor walks around and chats with employees. The simple format—(1) you performed like this, (2) the standard is this, (3) this is how we get you to perform to the standard, and (4) this is our follow-up plan—can be an exceptionally valuable five-minute conversation for the supervisor and employee. The simple format also is a great pattern for giving employees compliments. When giving an employee a compliment, you want to identify simply and precisely what the employee did well and why it was good, so that the employee can repeat the behavior and set a positive example for other employees. Finally, these sessions build great morale for a team. Employees, regardless of age, experience, or background, are motivated when a supervisor observes their work, comments on it, and shows them how to improve.

CHAPTER 18

VETERAN LESSON 18: POSITION YOURSELF FOR PROMOTION

Promotion and advancement in the military usually come after key jobs have been accomplished, requirements met for time in military rank, and military schools successfully completed. The military also lays out timelines, career counselors, positions to be achieved, and educational goals to be achieved so a person can be promoted into the next rank. There are none of these guidelines, career counselors, or even a corporate organizational design for an employee's promotion in the civilian world. You have to be aggressive and focused, employ initiative, consistently strive to be a better business leader, learn constantly, and be seamless in your production of results and promoting your abilities to senior management. You are responsible for your promotions.

Veterans Must Promote Themselves for Career Success

You have to learn the art of "intelligent self-promotion." Intelligent self-promotion is a subtle, indirect, fact-based, and action-driven campaign—for you to influence and sell key senior leaders on your skills, qualities, leadership, and demonstrated performance results—that is directed toward enhanced commercial responsibility. Your potential reward will be increased positional opportunities, additional pay and benefits, and the potential for more promotions. You must understand the key points of influence and subtlety to ensure a successful promotion process.

In the previous chapters, following the Understand, Plan, Execute, and Improve model of how you add value to a corporation, you learned how to assess the company's mission, customer base, competition, and operations. Your next logical step is to look at where you can add the most value to improving the company. This is a critical analysis, because it is the first step of using all your critical military skills and experience to start improving the company and, by extension, advancing your own career progression. Once you are producing financial, operational, and leadership results for the company, you need to think about how you can start to promote yourself for increased responsibility or into other business functions that support your own career plan. Remember, shameless self-promotion, in both the military and the commercial world, is viewed in a very negative context and will *not* assist you in receiving a promotion or being considered for a new opportunity.

Intelligent Self-Promotion for Your Career Advancement

You must use intelligent self-promotion to sell what you are doing for the company, how you are leading, and what you can do in the future for the company. There are three steps in the intelligent self-promotion process:

Step 1: Lay the foundation.
Step 2: Build the framework of success.
Step 3: Be aware of potential career pitfalls.

Step 1: Lay the Foundation

Intelligent self-promotion is not boastful, does not undercut others, is not unethical, and does not place the individual before the team. Rather, intelligent self-promotion places employees, their business results, their leadership skills, and their potential in an open and honest light in front of company and industry executives who make promotion decisions for their future career. In order to use intelligent self-promotion, you must lay the foundation for a successful self-promotion effort to advance your career prospects.

- **Leverage your skills.** You need to bring and leverage all of your military and commercial skills to improve your segment of the business and the abilities of the people that work with you. You need to lean on your military skill sets as a starting point but then quickly adapt your military skills to best meet the commercial challenges that involve you on a daily basis. You also need to get closely involved in new areas such as accounting, inventory management, and knowledge of the products and services, and you need to ensure that each member of your sales team is being compensated correctly within the company's bonus structure. You must leverage all of your skill sets, both military and commercial, and apply those effectively to your existing business challenges to leverage your entire background toward a promotion.
- **Utilize measures of effectiveness and financial results.** Business is all about hitting your numbers and demonstrating in a clear, honest, and concise fashion where your business results began, what you did to improve the results, and where the business measures ended up at the conclusion of your efforts. As a general rule of thumb, there will only be about 50% of the required metrics present for you to demonstrate sufficiently the positive effects that you are having on the business. The determination of what measures reflect your business success is never easy, but it is an absolute necessity for the business leader and team to determine that their strategy is a success. Finally, business

leaders must select only four to six metrics to reflect the success of their business. The use of more than six indicators reduces you from a businessperson to a data gatherer. Metrics are the indicators of success, but all efforts need to be focused on achieving the business plan to lead to improved results. The use of performance measures and success measures that employ good data and indicators that accurately reflect the performance of the business will demonstrate in clear and efficient terms the financial contributions, leadership contribution, and operational improvements brought about by your efforts.

- **Gather assessments of your leadership abilities.** In the military, most of the assessments of a soldier's leadership abilities come from direct superiors or an honest section sergeant or first sergeant, if that person is lucky. In the corporate world, using 360-degree leadership assessments and other similar tools, most of the assessments of business people's leadership abilities come from those that they lead—a welcome development. There are several important aspects to realize as you take a leadership position in the corporate world. The first is that the majority of people who are required to accomplish a business plan or task probably do not work for you directly. The vast majority of corporations are exceptionally flat in their structure, as opposed to the rigidly hierarchical military. Therefore, a leadership assessment gauging a person's team leadership skills is an absolute must. The second point is that people's title or position in the leadership structure does not reflect their true organizational power. In the military, a glance at a collar or body armor reveals a person's positional power. In a corporation, it is not nearly so clear. Leadership assessments can also help capture some of the subtleties of the corporate leadership structure and how you fit in. Finally, leadership assessments provide the most direct and invaluable perspective on what those who are led truly feel about a leader or potential leader. Business leaders must not be afraid to ask what others think of their leadership skills, and they must be unafraid to embrace and dedicate themselves to the change required to be a better leader.

Step 2: Build the Framework of Success

Once you have established the foundation of your career advancement through demonstration of your business results and a thorough understanding and assessment of your leadership abilities, you need to expand your knowledge of the company, industry best practices, and new commercial skill sets. Learning, new experiences, and expanding business knowledge are the hallmark of building the framework of a successful career advancement.

- **Stay abreast of your company's business results, the competition, the industry, and general business trends.** The Corporate Periodic Intelligence Report outlined the foundation for a thorough understanding of the competition and the industry environment. Great commercial leaders need to have an aggressive, constant, and insatiable quest for knowledge about their company, the competition, customers, their industry, and general business developments. The only way that commercial leaders can respond to this is by maintaining a strong personal network of contacts and by voracious reading of mainstream media such as *Business Week*, the *Wall Street Journal*, the *Financial Times*, the *New York Times*, *Fortune*, local media publications, specialty business publications such as *Adweek*, and bloggers who have a unique and respected following for their perspective on a product, service, or industry. The entire purpose of having the knowledge of your company, competition, industry, and business trends is to be able to understand and employ these ideas ahead of the competition and in advance of consumer preferences in order to generate the optimal product and service solutions. It is a near impossibility for people who do not have a thorough understanding of their company, industry, and business trends to build a solution of sustainable competitive value. Great commercial leaders understand and know their business and are never satisfied in their own knowledge base.

- **Learn and improve your commercial business skills.** You must be in a constant and consistent learning environment. Your military skill sets that you can successfully translate to use in business serve as a foundational level of business learning, but they are not a graduate business level of learning. The commercial landscape of products, customers, competition, legal issues, societal trends, internal company abilities, and technological abilities are in a constant state of change, and the rate of change is always increasing. Your sole offense against the dynamics of change in the marketplace and economic landscape is to continue to learn, know, and grow in your commercial skill sets. You need to use formal education, such as classes at local community and four-year colleges in subjects such as finance, accounting, statistics, operations, and marketing. Informal education plays an even greater role, through reading current newspapers, business magazines, industry journals, and general business periodicals. You must include nontraditional educational sources—such as blogs, conversations with customers, and observing customers in their product purchase and product usage behavior—to continue to grow and expand your business knowledge fully. Finally, pay close attention to the sharpest critics and contrarians for continuing business education. The contrarians are often the closest to the future trends in a business or industry.

- **Expand into new positions and skill sets outside of your comfort zone.** For the vast majority of veterans, it is remarkably easy to move into positions that reflect as closely as possible their old military positions. Although this makes excellent sense from an initial job hiring perspective, it makes very little sense from a long-term career perspective. Survey the biographies of any set of executives from any industry, and you will discover a breadth of experiences from operations to finance to marketing to customer service. Breadth and depth of experience make a great commercial business leader, and all of these executives, at one time or another, have had to step outside of their comfort zones into a new area or industry of experience. You need to keep a wide focus for career advancement opportunities and ensure that you look toward every area of the company where you can add value for your company's operations.

Step 3: Be Aware of Potential Career Pitfalls

Your quest for promotion could end up severely damaging your existing career and future prospects if pursued incorrectly. You have to handle your path toward promotion within the framework of the company culture, your abilities, and the economic environment. Your keys of corporate professionalism are to appear capable, ready, a team player, and willing to step up for a promotion. You must not appear overly ambitious, not a team player, or more concerned with yourself than the firm. Intelligent self-promotion is to advance your career, not destroy it through reckless behavior.

- **Stay balanced with work, family, and personal activities.** Time and satisfaction imbalances between work, family, and personal aspirations can throw your career and life into a tailspin. In the entire work life balance equation, you and your family must realize straight away that this must always be a goal. Moreover, when the work life balance is achieved, it is usually for a temporary period, because changes in the ages of children, their new activities, changes in family goals, and new career challenges again call for new demands in work and life balance. You need to strive constantly to ensure that your efforts are always dedicated toward a balance of your work, life, and personal activities. Just as in the military, when preparation for deployments and combat deployments demanded long work hours, business execution—with its deal building, financial analysis, negotiations, and new product development—also calls for long hours, focus, and dedication. There needs to be an ebb and flow for you to maintain your commitment and dedication to the success of the corporation but also maintain a higher level of commitment to your family and yourself. We all have worked long hours in the military and at work, but not one of us has yet to receive a hug or a word of encouragement from the office building as we go out the door. Success in business requires extraordinary commitment, but that commitment must fit with a balance of work, family, and personal life. Employees can maintain 100% job focus for a while, but, over time, they lose the focus, commitment, and education that they initially had from their support base of family and inner strength. You need to maintain a daily, weekly, and monthly structure, as much as possible, to keep your work and life in balance.
- **Stay on the lookout for new leaders, new companies, and new job opportunities by promoting yourself to key leaders.** You must have a broad perspective to advance your career, both within and outside of your existing company and industry. You are the person solely responsible for your career advancement. To prepare and position for career advancement, you need to look broadly through the company and the industry for opportunities. A great many of the opportunities, both by title and company, may initially appear to be beneath your current title and position. In the corporate world, the advancement style known as "checker-boarding" is a viable avenue for promotion and advancement. Checker-boarding occurs when an employee moves in a lateral or downward direction across an organization or industry in order to gather new skill sets, make new contacts, and increase his or her visibility and contribution within an organization. To the vast majority of veterans, who are used to a culture where the process of promotion is constantly and consistently upward, this may appear distasteful and seem like a demotion. However, corporate promotion is about constant demonstration of success in different position while always gaining new skill sets and more visibility to the company's executives. You have to exercise initiative, judgment, and an intense desire to achieve for this to advance your career fully.
- **Do a great job in your current position.** By far the number one best piece of career progression advice is to do and continue to do a great job in your current position. The old adage—that there are no small positions, only small

people—is as alive and true in the corporate world as in the military world. You need to excel and master your current profession, but then you need to look for ways to add greater commercial value beyond the confines of your existing position. Employees who have mastered their current position can do a number of tasks to demonstrate that they are prepared for additional responsibilities. Steps such as training a subordinate or subordinates to take over your position help create a sustainable succession plan for your position and make you able to be placed elsewhere quickly. Volunteering for additional responsibility demonstrates to executives that you are looking beyond the present position for new skills and challenges. Finally, creating a coaching or subordinate development program to expand the skill sets and career aspirations of junior employees readily demonstrates your ability to lead, as well as creating a "bench" of ready junior leaders for the organization. Mastering your existing position and then looking for new challenges, even in your current role, are crucial steps toward promotion.

Summary of the Use of Intelligent Self-Promotion to Position Yourself for Career Advancement

You are the sole person responsible for your career and career progression. That said, there are hundreds of people who are willing and agreeable to help veterans advance their career—from existing employees, interested executives, and complete strangers. You must adopt an intelligent self-promotion strategy to demonstrate concisely and concretely the positive results that you have brought to the business, create a lifelong love of learning and personal improvement to build a framework of success, and be highly observant of career pitfalls and detractors that may derail your plans. In addition, although the military path of career advancement is a linear, upward sloping path of promotions, schooling, and known and understood duty responsibilities; the path of civilian career advancement is anything but linear.

You must be open to lateral moves or even temporary demotions in order to build larger networks and gather critical business skills that are required for continuing success in the business. There is also a heightened sense of risk that may require frequent and far-reaching geographic moves that make the military pattern of two-to-three-year moves appear stable. Indeed, in some cases, you may need to change your company or companies in order to gather necessary skill sets, new responsibility, or take on a new venture to build toward a brighter career future. Additionally, you may change your employer or career multiple times, as you look for a profession, opportunity, and corporate culture that are a fit for your career aspirations, personality, and personal work preferences. Finally, you may discover in your career progression that a corporate lifestyle or particular corporate culture does not fit you. The path of entrepreneurship, starting your own business or nonprofit organization, may be a path of service that balances your career desires with your chosen lifestyle. For some military veterans, the opportunity to build and lead their own business is an irresistible combination of their skill sets and business desires.

All of these career progression examples, mixed with a challenging economic environment, highlight the potential, variability, and uniqueness of a civilian career progression compared to a military career linear path of advancement. You made things happen on the battlefield by employing your skills, passion, leadership, experience, education, and initiative. You can utilize these same skill sets in your companies and careers for your career progression and to build a better, more fulfilled life.

CHAPTER 19

VETERAN LESSON 19: USE MENTORING FOR CAREER IMPROVEMENT

Military people understand and embrace the role of mentorship. Mentoring is the act of helping people improve in some area of their professional or personal life that will help them advance quicker toward their professional goals. In the military, it was a common everyday occurrence for soldiers from all ranks to help each other succeed.

I remember, during some of the extremely chaotic days that followed the initial ground invasion in March 2003, a seasoned lieutenant colonel pulled me aside, closed the door, and began discussing with me, in a confident, reasonable, and respectful tone, the things that I needed to start doing—not only to plan better but to lead better, now that my 30-person planning team was fully engaged in a difficult combat environment that did not have an immediate end anywhere in sight. The session with the lieutenant colonel only took 30 minutes, but in that time, he laid out some great concepts and techniques for me to help lead a staff better in combat.

Mentoring relationships can come from senior leaders and junior team members and can involve an ongoing training relationship or a one-time skill improvement session. Mentoring improves relationships, makes the organization better, and improves individual skill sets. In a mentoring relationship, rank structure is set respectfully aside, and parties revert to the trainer and trainee roles. Mentorship in the military is best seen as a gift that is given from one soldier to another to increase skill sets and to make each one a more proficient soldier. It is an understood requirement that once you serve as a recipient of a mentor's time, you need to become a mentor for someone else.

Military Mentoring: A Proven Solution for Corporate Mentoring Programs

When military personnel become veterans, the ability to mentor, coach, and transform soldiers, marines, airmen, and sailors into skilled, efficient, and fully engaged corporate business leaders continues and takes on even greater importance. For a business, one of the primary tasks of human resource personnel is talent management. Talent management within a corporate organization is a simple concept: Hire, retain, promote, and develop the best possible employees that make the corporation financially successful.

You are of immense benefit to the talent management process of a corporation because, from your military experience, you are willing to take the time to develop and improve other veterans, potential new hires, and current employees. The greatest value that you can bring to other veterans is to take an active role in networking, mentoring, coaching, promoting, and hiring veterans. In your organization, you can also mentor, coach, develop, and hire other employees of talent. When you are an active mentor, you play a strategic role in the company because you are seeking to develop, retain, hire, and promote the best employees possible.

The Veteran Mentoring Process

The mentoring process can be a formal or informal process and is meant to provide senior business leaders with a forum to pass on their wisdom and learning points to younger business leaders. The mentoring relationship between the mentor and the mentee can be from a veteran to a veteran, a non-veteran to a veteran, or a veteran to a non-veteran. Any of these combinations work to help the corporation develop excellent talent and discover and build world-class talent.

Mentoring is a four-step process. The order of the steps is not strict, but following them helps mentees best identify what they want to achieve so they can use the mentor's time in the best possible fashion.

Steps in the Veteran Mentoring Process

Step 1. Set professional goals and identify possible mentors.
Step 2. Interview mentors and establish the mentoring relationship.
Step 3. Meet with mentor and determine action steps toward professional goals.
Step 4. Review progress and implement mentor guidance.

You can be either the mentor or the mentee. In either case, you should always strive to be a mentor within the corporation. You possess leadership, counseling, and motivational skills that are unmatched in the commercial sector. You play an important role in the talent management functions of a corporation. The ability to serve as a mentor or recognize areas of improvement to act as a mentee are essential contributions to a corporation's talent management. The following process assumes that you are the mentee, hoping to get the most out of the relationship.

Step 1: Set Professional Goals and Identify Possible Mentors

The first step in the mentoring process is to set professional goals. Professional goals can be firm objectives, such as becoming the vice president of sales by age 35 or gaining additional experience in operations. The professional goals section can include positions that you would like as well as different functional experiences. The sources to help determine professional goals are exceptionally broad. Biographies of senior C-level executives can be obtained from the company investor section of the website or through a simple Internet search. Personal discussions and research also yield clues, other professional positions, and various education paths to set professional goals. Finally, books, websites, magazines, newspapers, TV, blogs, and other media outlets offer insights into leading business executives, their backgrounds, and what they claim led to their success. Colleges, universities, and community colleges are also excellent places to look for skilled professionals with dynamic backgrounds. Many professionals start a second career teaching business, and their backgrounds can provide excellent structure for leadership skills.

Once you have a variety of sources for modeling a business leader, you need to select skills, positions, locations, or other industries that you wish to work with to help advance your career. For example, if you wish to advance toward a position as a chief financial officer (CFO), your progression in a company is usually marked by positions as a controller, working in the company's investor relations division, working in the company's merger and acquisitions (M&A) division, and several positions as the CFO for other separate business units (SBU) in the company.

The final part of step 1 is to select potential mentors. You will have identified skill sets and positions gained from modeling the careers and insights of other C-level business professionals within both your company and the industry. The next step is to find mentors within your company and the industry to help you reach your goals. To find a mentor, share your career goals with your immediate and next level boss and ask his or her opinion on two or three people to contact for a possible mentoring relationship. You should carry out this same process to help identify mentors by asking industry leaders and appropriate professional level educators about two or three leaders in their identified areas of improvement to contact for mentoring. You should identify approximately eight to ten potential mentors to contact for an initial interview.

Step 2: Interview Mentors and Establish the Mentoring Relationship

Once the potential mentors have been identified, contact them via a brief phone call or e-mail to ask for a meeting to discuss career development. You should conduct the initial meeting with the goal of introducing yourself, outlining your professional goals, and then judging the fit of your personality with the potential mentor.

You should share the major relevant career details, education, and professional achievements from your résumé with the potential mentor. An in-depth, full description of your entire career history is not required—just enough so the potential mentor gets a good feel and understanding of your qualifications. Next, discuss your career and professional goals in general terms that leave the discussion of these goals open to feedback from the potential mentor. Finally, engage in a good back and forth with the potential mentor, to discuss the best steps, positions, and educational steps to achieve your career goals. You should also identify potential personal character and professional business traits that need to be improved to meet your professional goals.

During the course of the meeting, you should be conducting a self-assessment of the potential mentor, as well as of the value of the potential mentor's advice to advance your commercial career. You should feel at ease with the potential mentor, feel the ability to be open and honest with professional questions, and feel that the potential mentor has adequate time in his or her schedule to be a mentor. Furthermore, you should consider schedules, geographic location, and possible conflicts of interest in the selection of a mentor. For example, the choice of a mentor who is a direct and close competitor of your current employer would not be a good choice of a mentor because of possible loyalty and conflicts of interest.

You probably need to ask potential mentors how often their schedule allows you to meet, if they can commit to a formal mentor-mentee relationship, or whether the relationship should be more informal. You should not be discouraged if the potential mentor chooses a less frequent and more informal relationship. The demands of work, family life, volunteer activities, and relaxation time are a continuous challenge for many executives. Instead, you should view the infrequent mentor as a resource gained and develop the relationship slowly and consistently. Once you and the potential mentor are agreed that this would be a good mentor-mentee relationship, you can work on a meeting and professional development schedule.

Step 3: Meet with the Mentor and Determine Action Steps toward Professional Goals

The meetings with the mentors should be brief, 30 to 60 minutes, and usually occur no more than one time a month. The meeting's brevity and frequency is driven by allowing mentees enough time to make progress toward their goals and by the mentees giving consideration for the time the mentors are spending with them. The meeting should be scheduled out for three to six months, to allow both the mentor and the mentee sufficient time to adjust their schedules and ensure that both have sufficient time to prepare and meet.

In advance of the mentor meeting, prepare a brief summary of what professional projects you have been working on, your progress toward the goals identified in step 1, and any roadblocks encountered. You should largely drive the meeting agenda to use the time to answer your development questions and ensure that the mentor's time is used productively. It is also helpful for you to bring along one or two major business articles to get the mentor's perspective on the business problem and application to your current corporation. As a note of caution, you should not reveal any company proprietary information, non-public financial results, or other insider information to a mentor outside of your company. Use the mentor's time to assess your progress on hard and soft business skills and what you need to be doing prior to the next meeting in order to move closer to your goal.

Step 4: Review Progress and Implement Mentor Guidance

You should prepare a running assessment on your progress every four to eight weeks, to inform your mentor on your progress toward the goals identified in step 1. Prepare an assessment of your progress prior to meetings, and then, afterward, update to the mentor on your current professional activities and explain your progress. The ability to have an open discussion about progress or lack of progress toward a professional goal is a vital attribute of the mentor-mentee relationship. If you or the mentor cannot be honest, the mentoring relationship will not succeed in improving your business skills.

You need to ask a great number of questions on how to improve your skills. This may be a potential area of discomfort for most veterans, because they are asking for direct, specific, and unvarnished feedback on how they can improve their professional skills. However, a little personal courage goes a long way toward developing yourself into an even better employee. The assessment of progress toward defined goals is a very important part of the mentoring relationship.

Summary

Mentoring is a fantastic, easy-to-achieve process for you to gain valuable knowledge toward the advancement of your career and to give back a substantial portion of your applicable military experience to advance other veterans and other employees of merit within the company. The bottom line goal and purpose of mentoring is to help employees identify their goals and then create a path for you to meet with senior executives to generate plans and advice for them to achieve their professional goals. Finally, veterans can be great mentors for other employees, from non-veterans to fellow veterans. Mentoring creates better employees and creates better business results for the corporation. You should simultaneously seek to be a mentor to improve other employees, as well as be a mentee, to ensure a solid advancement in your existing business skill sets.

CHAPTER 20

VETERAN LESSON 20: ADAPT MILITARY TOOLS TO COMMERCIAL BUSINESS APPLICATIONS

Different U.S. military branches of service, various military occupational specialties, military experiences, both combat and non-combat, combined with a wide range of commercial experiences, from finance to transportation to human resources, create a rich field to develop techniques and tools to bridge military experience to commercial use. Through all of this military experience, education, and commercial experience, there are nearly endless varieties of new techniques and procedures that can be adapted to the corporate business world. This book proposed only a few of the potential possibilities that are in the idea marketplace and that you can bring to your workplace.

When you decide to create a commercial improvement with a military technique or process, it is vital that these commercial adaptations of military practices follow a similar structure so that there is clear understanding, adaptation, testing, and planned implementation to support successful commercial business practices. Your challenge is to demonstrate adequately and precisely how a commercial process or problem can be solved through the utilization of a military technique or practice to meet commercial requirements. By following an outline of ten common steps, you can create this military-to-commercial transition process into a repeatable process that will enable you to anticipate possible benefits, problems, and solutions, as well as ensure that the process created meets the demands of the commercial marketplace and your company. Finally, there is not always a military process or procedure that cleanly meets the needs of a commercial process. However, using this process, a military process is fully tested for suitability to ensure that its implementation meets a commercial requirement.

Process Steps to Translate a Military Function to Support a Commercial Function

You need to have a consistent and established process to help navigate the transition of military processes and techniques to commercial processes and techniques. There are nine key steps to translate a military process to a commercial process (see Figure 20.1):

Step 1. Name and description of the military function
Step 2. Purpose of the military function
Step 3. The commercial problem statement or need
Step 4. The commercial measures of effectiveness to evaluate performance
Step 5. How the military function addresses the commercial need
Step 6. Commercial groups and individuals involved
Step 7. Testing plan for company approval
Step 8. Company implementation plan
Step 9. Implementation review and follow-up

Looking into your past military experience is a great way for you to expand the capabilities and talents that you bring to a commercial organization. However, there are definite pitfalls in the translation of a military process or procedures to a commercial organization. This nine-step process is to ensure that you have one of the following outcomes: (1) a successful direct translation of a military process to a commercial process, (2) an adaptation of a military process to a commercial process, or (3) an abandonment of an attempt to translate a military process to a commercial process. The abandonment of something that does not work prior to implementation is a good thing. Abandonment of an idea combines innovation, initiative, and good business sense—a great business trait! Finally, this process helps protect your good name and reputation. This process is designed to make a process prove itself prior to implementation so that you do not try to implement a new commercial process that does not achieve the commercial objective.

Step 1: Name and Description of the Military Function

The first step in the process to translate a military function to a commercial function is to have a good, simple grasp of the military procedure. The grasp of the military procedure or process is essential so that you understand all aspects of resources required, the number and training of the people involved, how the military process works from start to finish, and what are some of the possible problems and solutions involved. Additionally, a detailed experience level with the military process is a great benefit for the planning, training, and implementation of the process. This step should include a play-by-play description of the military process to include all relevant personnel, resources required, and any other pertinent details.

Step 2: Purpose of the Military Function

The second step is a very brief description, in one or two sentences, of the purpose of the military function or process. For example, if you were considering adopting the military practice of a medical evacuation (MEDEVAC) SOP for your building construction worksite to ensure a safe work practice, the purpose of the military MEDEVAC SOP would be as follows.

The purpose of the military MEDEVAC SOP is to ensure that all personnel know the steps to take for the immediate alert of medical ambulance personnel to the location,

Military to Commercial Tool Adaptation Worksheet

Military to Commercial Adaptation Step 1: Name and description of the military function.   As of: _____

Military Tool or Processes:

Military to Commercial Adaptation Step 2: Purpose of the military function.

Purpose and Objective of the Military Function:

Military to Commercial Adaptation Step 3: The commercial mission statement or need.

Commercial Process Mission Statement:
WHO:
WHAT:
WHEN:
WHERE:
WHY:

Military to Commercial Adaptation Step 4: The commercial measures of effectiveness or success measures.

	Name	Definition	Data Source	Frequency	Unit of Measure	Remarks
Measure 1						
Measure 2						
Measure 3						

Military to Commercial Adaptation Step 5: How the military function addresses the commercial need.

How the Military Function Addresses the Commercial Need:

Military to Commercial Adaptation Step 6: Commercial groups and individuals involved.

Commercial Groups and Individuals Involved:

Military to Commercial Adaptation Step 7: The new process to adapt the military function to the commercial function.

The New Commercial Processes (Combination of Military and Existing Commercial Process):

Military to Commercial Adaptation Step 8: New process testing plan for company approval.

	Time Period +1	Time Period +2	Time Period +3	Time Period +4	Time Period +5	Time Period +6	Time Period +7	Time Period +8	Time Period +9
Group 1									
Group 2									
Group 3									
Measure 1									
Measure 2									
Measure 3									

Military to Commercial Adaptation Step 9: Company implementation plan.

Company New Process Implementation Plan:

Military to Commercial Adaptation Step 10: Implementation review and follow-up.

	Time Period +1	Time Period +2	Time Period +3	Time Period +4	Time Period +5	Time Period +6	Time Period +7	Time Period +8	Time Period +9
Group 1									
Group 2									
Group 3									
Measure 1									
Measure 2									
Measure 3									

Figure 20.1 Military to Commercial Tool Adaptation Worksheet.

condition, and quantity of injured personnel to ensure rapid, safe, and efficient evacuation of injured personnel to nearest medical facilities.

This simple sentence clearly lays out the purpose and goal of the military function. If a military process cannot be spelled out in one or two sentences, pause and regroup on the overall applicability of the military process for commercial use.

Step 3: The Commercial Problem Statement or Need

The commercial problem statement or commercial need statement can follow the military mission statement attributes of who, what, when, where, and why. The use of the mission statement attributes clearly outlines the commercial requirements in a simple, clear, and understandable format. A well-understood commercial need is essential to understand and match the military process to the commercial need. The description and explanation of the commercial problem statement components are as follows:

Who: The division of the company or business team involved.

What: A description of the business problem or process to be solved and its current performance level.

When: The date of planned implementation and how often the new process would be used (hourly, daily, weekly, etc.).

Where: The locations where the new process will be used.

Why: The overall goal of the commercial process and what it is trying to achieve. The use of cost-cutting goals, revenue generation goals, customer satisfaction goals, or defect reduction goals is all helpful to provide an improved level of clarity.

Step 4: The Commercial Measures of Effectiveness to Evaluate Performance

Measures or effectiveness are normally quantitative measurements, taken in hourly, daily, weekly, or monthly increments, that accurately depict how well a process is performing. For example, an ATM machine's operating software most likely has a default measure of effectiveness for how accurately it dispenses cash withdrawals. If I request $100 and the ATM gives me $100, the machine is working properly. However, if I request $100 and I am given $110 or $90, an accuracy error has occurred. For the ATM machine's operation, any error, even one, would prompt the ATM machine to shut down.

The commercial measures of effectiveness are essential to understand for a number of reasons. First, they provide a baseline as to how the existing commercial process is evaluated today so you can fully understand how the process has performed in the past. Second, the commercially adapted military process must ensure that it makes the designated commercial measures of effectiveness better than the existing process. If the new process does not improve the measures of effectiveness or makes them worse, the entire process is a failure. Third, the measures of effectiveness should have a strong relationship with values and items that are important to the customer. Finally, there should be at most two or three measures of effectiveness to evaluate the process. If more than three measures are used, the complexity of the measurement process, data requirements, and data updates can quickly become a burden to track, and it may be difficult to ensure that the new process is performing correctly and successfully. The selection of one to three good measures of effectiveness is the best way to evaluate a process and ensure, over time, that it is working correctly.

Step 5: How the Military Function Addresses the Commercial Need

This is the combination of Step 1, the description of the military process, with Step 3, the description of the commercial need. The combination of the information in these two steps yields how the military process meets the commercial process requirements. This should be a detailed, systematic process description of how the military process is adapted and modified to achieve the "why" in Step 3 of the commercial need statement. This should be a very detailed description of personnel involved, specific actions to take, when to take the specified action, and the result of the action to meet the requirements of the commercial need statement. Finally, the measures of effectiveness identified in Step 4 should be used to ensure that the new process is successful. This should be detailed enough to meet the commercial requirements, but not so detailed as to make the process unwieldy or confusing to the actors.

Step 6: Commercial Groups and Individuals Involved

This is a list of all the commercial individuals and organizations that have to agree on the new process, coordinate with the new process, or be trained on the new process so that the new military-to-commercial process can be used within the organization. This list should be all encompassing; it is used to create the approval plan, the implementation plan, and the training plan. You should create three groups to help in the communication and implementation of the new process. There should be a group that needs to approve the process, a group for coordination that needs to be aware of the new process, and a group that needs to be trained on the new process. Any supporting groups or individuals should also be included, such as budgeting, resources, or major customer groups that could be affected by the change in the existing commercial process.

Step 7: Testing Plan for Company Approval

Once the military process has been adapted to meet the commercial requirements, you need to start a sales campaign to the three groups identified in Step 6— to sell the merits of the idea and to receive permission to create a pilot or test program of the new process to demonstrate its value to the organization. The sales campaign to the three groups—the approval group, the coordination group, and the training group identified in Step 6—needs to be a simple presentation or demonstration. The sales campaign presentation should show the existing process, if one exists, show the new process, and then, using the measures of effectiveness and other descriptions, show how the new process will be better. The final portion of the sales campaign presentation is to request permission to have a pilot or a test of the new process and to re-emphasize the benefits of the new process for the organization. In some organizations, employees do not have to ask permission, they can just conduct a pilot and share the results of the pilot.

Upon approval of the pilot for the new process, you need to use selectively the planning tools of the synchronization matrix and other tools to arrange for the training and implementation steps for the pilot. You should spend a great deal of time in informing, selling, educating, demonstrating, and proving the value of the new process before, during, and after the implementation of the pilot. The success of the pilot makes the full-scale implementation of the new process much easier. The demonstrated successful pilot is crucial to selling the entire organization on the new process. You need to ensure that the pilot is small enough yet representative enough to be a good test of the new process. If the pilot process fails, the entire organization is not threatened and you can go back to step 1 to redo the process and learn from the mistakes. If the pilot succeeds, you can decide to do a bigger pilot or go for full implementation of the new process.

The final step in the pilot process is to conduct a commercial AAR to look for ways to improve the process tested in the pilot and to take the sales campaign back on the road throughout the organization to demonstrate the results, learning points, and the request for full implementation of the new process. The demonstration of the success of the pilot is vitally important so that the new process can maintain its momentum and fully demonstrate to any naysayers that the new process works. Nothing speaks to the success of a project more than a successful pilot.

Step 8: Company Implementation Plan

Just as in the case of the pilot project implementation plan, you need to take the implementation plan on the road to demonstrate the pilot results (to reassure and convince skeptics), propose their initial implementation plan, and gather feedback from everyone involved on the necessary changes to the proposed implementation plan. This implementation plan should only ask direct permission for implementation from the person(s) or group(s) with the final authority to make the change. There are always skeptics and persons who resist change. The use of a pilot, gathering feedback through the commercial AAR, and gathering feedback on the implementation plan is the best way to convince and disarm skeptics, showing them that this plan will work. Additionally, through their inclusion in the commercial AAR and implementation planning, people are far more likely to feel included and part of the change process.

The implementation plan needs to focus heavily on the use of the synchronization matrix, formal and informal training, and any other necessary pilots to ensure that the implementation plan will be a success. Additionally, by using transparent, open, and publicly shared measures of effectiveness, you create excitement and buy-in from the whole organization as the new process takes effect. The old saying is very true: "success has many fathers." An implementation plan that gathers and incorporates feedback from others and shares the responsibility of a successful implementation has a much greater chance of long-term success.

Finally, the implementation plan should incorporate the systematic use of the commercial AAR process throughout the implementation so that any problems can be determined immediately and a solution can be put in place to prevent a problem early on in the plan extending throughout the implementation.

Step 9: Implementation Review and Follow-Up

Most project fails over the long term because, after good planning, a successful pilot, and a thorough implementation, they do not have a long term follow-up process to ensure that the new process remains in effect and successful. The use of the measures of effectiveness viewed on a weekly or monthly basis, combined with a quarterly commercial AAR, is an essential step to keep the new process effective and functioning. The measures of effectiveness demonstrate that the process is working, and the commercial AAR helps identify any trends or new requirements from the employees who execute the process. Finally, the business environment, customer requirements, and competitor actions are exceptionally dynamic, and a change in any one of the areas of the business environment may necessitate a change in the process. This change in the business environment may require a process redesign, the selection of new measures of effectiveness, or the introduction of the process to a new group of employees.

Summary of Steps to Adapt Military Tools to Commercial Application

As veterans, you can become great innovators within your organizations when you start to look into how you can leverage your entire experience base, military and commercial experience, to improve existing processes and solve old problems within your businesses and organizations. The systematic process to translate military processes into a commercial use is detailed, but it helps you fully understand the commercial problem, understand the military process, understand how to measure the success of the new process, test the new process before implementation, and then create a detailed implementation and follow-up plan to ensure success.

Commercial organizations are very similar to the military in that everyone hates a new process, especially one that fails. Often, there is only a one-time opportunity to create a change, and a new process that fails implementation usually does not resurface ever. Additionally, a successful new process design, pilot implementation, and full company implementation represent a great opportunity for you to make a great name for yourself and set yourself up for new opportunities and further challenges. The military experience base is a great asset, one that few commercial employees have, and you can use the successful translation of military-to-commercial business practices as a springboard to a more successful career.

SECTION 5

SUMMARY

You will create exceptional value for the company you work for when you bring the full range of your military training and experience to address the full range of commercial challenges confronting your company. As a military veteran, the keys to your being able to add instant value to the success of the company you work for (or wish to work for) is to follow the proven methodology of *Combat Leader to Corporate Leader*: (1) understand, (2) plan, (3) execute, and (4) improve.

Understand	Plan
Veterans Building Businesses, Employees, and Themselves for Commercial Success	Create a Corporate Periodic Intelligence Report
Military Ethics and Values Form the Foundation for Business Success	Understand Your Company Mission Statement
Maintain a Personal Improvement Plan	Use the War Game Process
Build Networks of Experts	Use the Military Synchronization Matrix
Overcome Common Mistakes Veterans Make in the Workplace	Employ Risk Mitigation

Execute	Improve
Employ Standard Operating Procedures (SOPs)	Use the Military After-Action Review
Back-Up Plans to Ensure Success	Employ Counseling Sessions
Create and Lead Powerful Teams	Position Yourself for Promotion
Use Military Crisis-Management Techniques	Use Mentoring for Career Improvement
Prepare an Exit Strategy	Adapt Military Tools to Commercial Business Applications

Each of these four areas is vital and important for you to be a competent, effective, and ethical businessperson. Understanding is the first area of importance, because business leaders must know themselves, the market, important industry leaders, and common mistakes in order to provide context and understanding to their decisions, while maintaining a strong sense of personal ethics and self-improvement. Planning is the next area of importance, because the use of systematic intelligence about the industry, competition, and customer preferences—combined with tools to synchronize business assets, anticipate problems, and mitigate risk—are essential to seeing a business plan and business strategy to a successful conclusion. Execution is best when it seeks to create powerful teams to empower successful operations that reduce variability using common processes, back-up plans, and anticipating how to prevent failure. Improvement is the final step for you to seek actively to improve other veterans, fellow employees, and business operations that position you for promotion.

CHAPTER 21

SUMMARY: THE 20 LESSONS THAT BRING THE GREATEST VALUE TO YOUR COMPANY AND CAREER

You must bring the full value of your military experience to your new civilian occupation in order to become a superior employee. The value of your veteran experience is more than your period of service to the country and the inherent positive occupational characteristics of ethics, hard work, leadership, dedication, and world-class technical skills. From day one, you must strive to employ all your military experience and military training to helping your new employer succeed in business. Employers from small business to *Fortune 500* employers recognize and sincerely appreciate you as veterans, for your years of dedication, combat service, exposure to personal danger, and sacrifice that you have paid and continue to pay for the defense of the country. However, corporations and organizations must succeed in the marketplace so they can continue to provide products to their customers, jobs to their employees, returns to the shareholders, and service to the communities in which they reside. Patriotism alone does not pay bills or achieve financial results.

Employers have obligations to their shareholders, current employees, communities, and customers to operate the best, most successful business with the best employees possible. Employers cannot hire you for your service alone, despite the incredibly high level of appreciation that employers have for veterans. Companies in every industry are challenged on a daily basis with operating the best, most efficient, and most profitable companies to offer excellent products and services. This is equally true for a 50,000-person company building world-class software as it is for a five-person company offering a pizza delivery service. Businesses today live, operate, and potentially fail in an era of speed, intense competition, demanding customers, cost pressures, and very little room for strategic error. Given this critical focus on business success, there are no better employees to guarantee success for any size business than veterans who employ their full range of military experience and who are dedicated to achieving commercial success.

You have a great deal to bring to the success of the company and organization for which you work. As veterans, you may believe that your biggest quality as employees is dedication or hard work, but this severely discounts the immediate business value that your military experience and training bring to your employer. You have operated successfully in a combat environment where mental agility, dedication, hard work, and a mastery of skills led you to victory on the battlefield. The military experience and military training that you possess make you a direct asset to your organization because of the leadership, planning, and execution skills that you bring. The point of the competitive advantage that you bring as a veteran is the successful application of your full range of military skill, experience, and education to solve business problems successfully and profitably. Your military skills and leadership as combat leaders work for you to become a successful corporate leader in the business world.

The following list shows the reasons why most employers and veterans like to hire and retain veterans.

Conventional Wisdom: Veteran Employment Characteristics

    (1) Dependability
    (2) Leadership and teamwork skills
    (3) Loyalty
    (4) Value-based work performance
    (5) Strong work ethic
    (6) Good technical skills
    (7) A proven record of accomplishment to operate successfully under stress
    (8) Ability to master new tasks and skill sets quickly
    (9) Comfort with authority and hierarchical work relationships
  (10) Intellectual and physical agility to adapt to a shifting work and competitive environment

In addition to the preceding list, the true range of value that you possess goes far beyond the seemingly traditional value points of positive workforce characteristics. The true points of business value that you bring are the skill sets to understand, plan, execute, and improve the companies you work for, which shapes, grows, and improves your companies for the future. The ability to shape and to maintain a better company is driven by the creation of procedures, understanding, and employee development that allow you, as a veteran, to become part of a workforce culture that becomes a sustainable competitive advantage for the company.

The 20 Lessons of Veteran Value for Commercial Business Excellence

    Lesson 1: The ability to understand the complete value that you as veterans bring to the workplace, with an understanding of what a business requires to be successful.
    Lesson 2: Action-based and ethical core values that support a profitable and effective business.

Lesson 3: The ability to create an individual, self-styled personal improvement plan to become a better businessperson.

Lesson 4: The ability to create personal networks to expand influence and understanding of major business issues in your company and industry.

Lesson 5: The ability to understand what causes you as veterans to be less effective in the workforce and how to prevent becoming a less effective employee.

Lesson 6: The ability to create a systematic, scheduled report on the marketplace, customers, and competition that helps the business remain competitive.

Lesson 7: The ability to dissect a company's mission statement to determine the core functions and responsibilities that the company needs to execute to be successful.

Lesson 8: The ability to test and refine business plans, using the commercial war game process, to create a plan more likely to anticipate the competition and succeed.

Lesson 9: The ability to synchronize all elements of a business plan to ensure the successful execution of a commercial plan and the optimal use of resources.

Lesson 10: The ability to use the risk assessment process to mitigate business risks, ensure safe operations, and to ensure a more successful commercial outcome.

Lesson 11: The ability to define and design key business processes into SOPs to allow businesses to excel at routine activities.

Lesson 12: The ability to use multiple back-up plans to ensure the successful operation of company critical tasks.

Lesson 13: The ability to form, lead, and be a member of a team in order to create successful and productive work groups.

Lesson 14: The ability to use military crisis management techniques to help keep a business on track during a crisis.

Lesson 15: The ability to ensure that business plans and operations have an exit strategy, and incorporate preventative steps to reduce the likelihood of a business plan failure.

Lesson 16: The ability to use the commercial AAR process to improve the success of company operations.

Lesson 17: The ability to use the employee performance counseling session to improve the productivity, efficiency, and job satisfaction of all employees.

Lesson 18: The ability to move up, lead, and gain more responsibility within the organization to advance your career.

Lesson 19: The ability to recruit, mentor, and retain other veterans to grow their skill sets and make them better employees for the company.

Lesson 20: The ability to adapt other military skill sets to commercial plans to ensure maximum use of military experience and training to solve commercial problems.

From the very beginning of your employment, you must represent yourself as more than just an average employee. The challenge for you as veterans is that you must be aggressive in representing the comprehensive commercial value that you bring to the workforce by openly educating and demonstrating your full range of commercial skills to employers. The true value of employees to a business is apparent when they fully maximize all of their education, skills, and experience, including military, to bring about a good commercial outcome. Good commercial outcomes are profitable, increase customer satisfaction, are cost-effective, fulfill a unique customer need, and are repeatable by the company. When you as a veteran apply your skills to these good commercial outcomes, both you and the company succeed.

From the initial hiring session, you must begin to define and differentiate yourself with the true and full commercial value that you bring to the corporation from the skill sets listed previously. Employers, when they have an employment candidate or employee, quickly realize the full value that a veteran brings—from both the traditional reasons to hire a veteran and the 20 true points of business value. Two of the most sought-after employee characteristics today are agility and versatility— that is, being able to accomplish the business mission in a diverse, sometimes confused, and constantly shifting business environment. As veterans, you excel at the type of mental and physical agility that leads to improved performance and superior business results.

You are of exceptional value within commercial and nonprofit organizations because you have the inherent understanding, planning, executing, and improving skills to take yourself and your organization to the next level of organizational performance. You are uniquely suited for success because you have had the understanding, planning, executing, and improving skills tested under extreme conditions and have emerged successful. Very few commercial business leaders are tested with the duration, ferocity, and variability as military leaders and military service members. You need to build upon this intense level of experience by pairing the wisdom and confidence from the tests of the battlefield with your adaptation of military skills and education to business problems. This combination is that of skilled leaders, who can understand the business environment, plan to take full effect of their company's strengths and competitor weaknesses, execute the business plan to ensure success despite challenges, and then create an action plan to improve future results and employee business performance. Veterans who take this approach to business will be successful in the marketplace and for the organizations for which they work.

20-LESSON SYNOPSIS

Understand

Lesson	Military Tool or Process	Commercial Business Use	Process Steps
1	The education, training, and experience of military personnel create great results	Military veterans are ideal employees to help businesses achieve success, due to their ability to leverage their military experience in their new career	**Military Qualities of Excellence** 1. Intelligence 2. Planning and preparation 3. Execution 4. Team leadership 5. Subordinate development 6. Technical skills **Commercial Qualities of Excellence** 1. Strategy 2. Execution 3 Financial results 4. Service and quality 5 Leadership 6. Consistent improvement
2	Military ethics and values	Commercial adaptation of military ethics and values for honest business practices	**Military Ethics and Values** 1. Ethics and values 2. Leadership by example 3. Leading from the front 4. Seeing the battlefield 5. Honesty and integrity 6. Imagination and anticipation 7. The will to win 8. Quality 9. Winning with humility 10. Concern for others
3	Military personnel staying in shape, developing, and prepared to accomplish mission	A military veteran must maintain a personal improvement plan for greater career success	**Military Veteran Personal Improvement Plan** 1. Internal—Positive, constructive attitude 2. Internal—Cognitive and physical well-being 3. Internal—Continued professional education 4. Internal—Openness to new experiences 5. External—Personal appearance 6. External—Professional decorum 7. External—Professional language 8. External—Example setting
4	Military-to-civilian career transition	Creating a network of experts to support your career success	**Network Creation Steps** 1. Determining what you want to know or accomplish 2. Determining whom to contact 3. Background research for the networking session 4. Conducting the networking session 5. Following up after the networking session
5	Military-to-civilian career transition	Overcome common mistakes veterans make in the workplace	**Common Mistakes Veterans Make in the Workplace** 1. Leaning on the past and not pushing toward the future 2. Treating others based upon your past rank and position 3. Not adjusting military presentation, bearing, and speech style to the corporate world 4. Letting yourself get too far away from military appearance, grooming, and fitness standards 5. Not asking or giving help to aid in the career transition 6. Not fully understanding the potential pitfalls of corporate culture 7. Not maintaining the can-do attitude

Plan

Lesson	Military Tool or Process	Commercial Business Use	Process Steps
6	Military intelligence report	Corporate periodic intelligence report to understand market, customers, competition, and technology	**Corporate Periodic Intelligence Report (CPIR) Elements** 1. Executive summary of findings and conclusion 2. Economic conditions 3. The competition 4. Customers 5. Industry developments 6. Emerging technology and practices 7. Coverage period for CPIR 8. A note of caution on the use of competitive intelligence
7	Military mission statement	Commercial mission statement analysis to understand the full scope of the company activities	**Military-to-Commercial Mission Statement Process** 1. Who—The commercial organization to carry out the business plan 2. What—The business objective to be accomplished 3. When—The deadline or goal for the business plan to be accomplished 4. Where—The market geographies or primary target markets for the business plan 5. Why—The overall purpose to be achieved by a successful business plan 6. Supporting steps and actions to accomplish mission statement—The necessary steps that the business must accomplish to fulfill its mission statement
8	Military war game planning process	Commercial war game process to test the plan against the competition	**The Commercial War Game Process** 1. Prepare for the war game 2. Execute the initial phase of the friendly business plan and determine the most likely competitor reaction 3. Friendly counteraction to offset the effectiveness of the competitor reaction 4. Supplement the draft business plan with the successful friendly action and counteractions from the war game 5. Formal and informal war game 6. Common mistakes in war game
9	Military synchronization matrix	Synchronize all company assets to effectively coordinate business plan execution	**Commercial Synchronization Matrix Steps** 1. Identify resources available to support the business plan 2. Identify major weekly events in business plan 3. Meet with all business resources to coordinate use in the business plan 4. Follow up to ensure implementation success
10	Military risk assessment process	Commercial risk management process to mitigate effects of uncontrolled risk	**Military to Commercial Risk Mitigation Process** 1. Identify the business objective 2. Identify the primary risks to the business objective 3. Identify the likelihood and the severity of the risk 4. Create a plan to implement the risk mitigation steps

Execute

Lesson	Military Tool or Process	Commercial Business Use	Process Steps
11	Military standard operating procedures (SOP)	Employ standard business process to improve business efficiency	**The Business SOP Creation Process** 1. Define the task, the purpose of the task, and how to measure its success 2. Create an SOP of who, what, when, where, and how to complete the task 3. Rehearse and revise the SOP to perfect who, what, when, where, and how to complete the task 4. Implement the SOP and incorporate it into operations and training 5. Schedule periodic SOP revision meetings (quarterly) to ensure the SOPs are as effective as possible
12	Military PACE contingency planning	Create back-up plans to ensure success of critical business functions	**The PACE Contingency Planning Process** 1. Primary back-up plan 2. Alternate back-up plan 3. Contingency back-up plan 4. Emergency back-up plan
13	Military team leadership principles	Leading business teams to commercial success	**Military-to-Business Team Leadership Process Steps** 1. Establish and communicate a strategic vision 2. Collaborate with the team to create a winning plan 3. Praise publicly, develop employees privately, and seek feedback from all 4. Develop others as leaders for their career success
14	Military crisis management techniques	Managing a corporate crisis to keep the business on track	**Military-to-Business Crisis Management Process Steps** 1. Identify that a crisis is occurring 2. Employ an open leadership and communication style 3. Maintain a confident and humble demeanor 4. Anticipate follow-on crisis events and ensure solid execution of crisis mitigation steps
15	Planning a strategic withdrawal	Commercial "exit" planning to identify plan weak points and identify when to exit a business strategy	**Commercial Exit Strategy Process Steps** 1. Determine measures of effectiveness to establish business plan performance 2. Create a "watch list" of customer, competition, and industry trends that could derail the business plan and strategy 3. Create three scenarios of possible events that would have low, medium, and high severity for the success of the business plan 4. Identify solutions to mitigate effects on company external and internal areas 5. Identify conditions for each scenario that would trigger a strategic exit and how to implement 6. Personal career management— ensure you have a well-described exit strategy for your career

Improve

Lesson	Military Tool or Process	Commercial Business Use	Process Steps
16	Military after-action review	Commercial after-action review to improve business operations	**Commercial After-Action Review Steps** 1. Establish an environment for review and introspection 2. Provide a brief overview of what happened and divide the operation into segments 3. Identify strengths, weaknesses, and recommendations for improvement in each business function 4. Create an action plan for improvement and follow up to ensure the improvements are happening
17	Military personnel performance counseling	Employee performance counseling to improve employee performance	**Employee Performance Counseling Steps** 1. Set the counseling stage 2. Describe the employee's performance and the company's accepted standards of performance 3. Evaluate the employee's performance and create an action plan to improve 4. Make the counseling a success: follow up, motivate, assist, and keep on track

18	Intelligent self-promotion	Employee positioning for promotion and additional corporate responsibilities	**Intelligent Self-Promotion Steps for Career Advancement**
			1. Lay the foundation
			  A. Leverage your skills
			  B. Utilize measures of effectiveness and financial results
			  C. Gather assessments of your leadership abilities
			2. Build the framework of success
			  A. Stay abreast of your company's business results, the competition, the industry, and general business trends
			  B. Learn and improve your commercial business skills
			  C. Expand into new positions and skill sets outside of your comfort zone
			3. Be aware of potential career pitfalls
			  A. Stay balanced with work, family, and personal activities
			  B. Stay on the lookout for new leaders, new companies, and new job opportunities by promoting yourself to key leaders
			  C. Do a great job in your current position

19	Military personnel development	Employee mentoring and development	**The Military Veteran Employee Mentoring Process** 1. Set professional goals and identify possible mentors 2. Interview mentors and establish the mentoring relationship 3. Meet with mentor and determine action steps toward professional goals 4. Review progress and implement mentor guidance
20	To be determined military process	Translating a military process to fulfill business requirements and commercial needs	**Military-to-Commercial Adaptation Steps** 1. Name and describe the military function 2. Purpose of the military function 3. The commercial problem statement or need 4. The commercial measures of effectiveness to evaluate performance 5. How the military function addresses the commercial need 6. Commercial groups and individuals involved 7. Testing plan for company approval 8. Company implementation plan 9. Implementation review and follow-up

BIBLIOGRAPHY

Baumann, Robert F.; Gawrych, George W.; and Kretchik, Walter E. *Armed Peacekeepers in Bosnia*, Combat Studies Institute Press, Fort Leavenworth, Kansas, 2004, pages 203–208.

Garamone, Jim, "4th Infantry Captures Saddam near Tikrit," American Forces Press Service dated December 14, 2003, on http://www.defendamerica.mil/articles/dec2003/a121403b.html, accessed on 5/25/2009.

Greenberg, Greg A., and Rosenbeck, Robert A. "Are Male Veterans at Greater Risk for Nonemployment Than Nonveterans?" *Monthly Labor Review*, United States Department of Labor, Washington, DC, Volume 130, Number 12, December 2007, pages 23–32.

Procter and Gamble Purpose, Values, and Principles statement, on http://www.pg.com/ company/who_we_are/ppv.shtml, accessed May 13, 2009.

Stewart, Richard W., *Staff Operations: The X Corps in Korea, December 1950*, Combat Studies Institute Press, Fort Leavenworth, Kansas, April 1991.

Storlie, Chadwick W., Letter to the Editor—Company Command, *Army Magazine*, Arlington, VA, August 2009, pages 6–8.

United States Government Census Bureau, *Current Population Survey (CPS) Description of Military Veteran Unemployment 1995–2008*, Bureau of Labor Statistics, United States Department of Labor, Washington, DC, accessed June 10, 2009.

Walker, James A., "Employment Characteristics of Gulf War-Era II Veterans in 2006: A Visual Essay," *Monthly Labor Review*, United States Department of Labor, Washington, DC, Volume 131, Number 5, May 2008, pages 3–13.

INDEX

Note: All page numbers followed by an *f* refer to figures on the designated page.

ABOUT THE AUTHOR

CHAD STORLIE has had a distinguished career in both military and civilian service. Chad is a U.S. Army Reserve Special Forces Lieutenant Colonel with 19 years of service in infantry, special forces, and joint headquarters units. He has served in Iraq, Bosnia, Korea, and throughout the United States. He has been awarded the Bronze Star, the Combat Infantryman's Badge, the Meritorious Service Medal, the Special Forces Tab, and the Ranger Tab. Chad is a mid-level marketing executive and has worked in marketing and sales roles for various companies, including General Electric, Comcast, and Manugistics.

In his spare time, Chad has taught marketing at Creighton University, developed Combat Analytics—a counterinsurgency assessment process—and written articles that have been published in several military journals. Chad holds a BA from Northwestern University and an MBA from Georgetown University. Chad lives in the Midwest with his wife and children.

Learn more at www.combattocorporate.com.